PUBLISHER COMMENTA

This manual is composed of four volumes, each containing its
are printed here. The purpose of the overall manual, in accord~~ance with the authority in DoD~~
Directive (DoDD) 5143.01, is to implement policy established in DoDD 5205.07, assign
responsibilities, and provide security procedures for DoD SAP information.

Volume 1. General Procedures - Assigns responsibilities, implements policy established in
DoD Instruction (DoDI) 5205.11, and describes the general procedures for the administration
of DoD SAP security.

Volume 2. Personnel Security - Assigns responsibilities and provides procedures for
personnel security for DoD SAPs.

Volume 3. Physical Security - Implements policy established in DoD Instruction (DoDI)
5205.11.

Volume 4. Marking - Provides guidance and procedures for the application of control
markings on DoD SAP information consistent with Executive Order 13526, Part 2001 subpart
C of title 32, Code of Federal Regulations, and Volume 2 of DoD Manual 5200.01.

Many of the books published by 4th Watch Publishing Co. are directly applicable to the subject
of national security. These publications cover a wide range of topics that are carefully designed
to work together to produce a holistic approach to security primarily for government agencies
and constitute the best practices used by industry. This holistic strategy to security covers the
gamut of security subjects from development of secure encryption standards for communication
and storage of information while at rest to how best to recover from a cyber-attack. If there is a
title you would like to see printed, please go to https://usgovpub.com and tell us.

Why buy a book you can download for free? We print this so you don't have to.

Some documents are only distributed in electronic media. Some online docs are missing some
pages or the graphics are barely legible. When a new standard is released, an engineer prints it
out, punches holes and puts it in a 3-ring binder. While this is not a big deal for a 5 or 10-page
document, many cyber documents are over 100 pages and printing a large document is a
time-consuming effort. So, an employee that's paid $50 an hour is spending hours simply
printing out the tools needed to do the job. That's time that could be better spent doing work.
We publish these documents so employees can focus on what they were hired to do.

Some of the other titles we print:

DoDM 5200.01	DoD Information Security Program
DoDI 5200.02	DoD Personnel Security Program
DoDI 1400.25	Civilian Personnel Management
DoDM 5220.22	National Industrial Security Program (NISP)
P5060.20	Marine Corps Drill and Ceremonies Manual
MCWP 3-11.1	Infantry Company Operations
MCRP 3-30.7	Commander's Tactical Handbook
Military Dictionary	DOD Dictionary of Military and Associated Terms
MIL-HNDBK 1013/1a	Design Guidelines for Physical Security of Facilities
MIL-HDBK-232A	RED/BLACK Engineering-Installation Guidelines
MIL-HDBK 1195	Radio Frequency Shielded Enclosures
TM 5-601	Supervisory Control and Data Acquisition (SCADA) Systems for C4ISR Facilities
MIL-HDBK 1012/1	Electronic Facilities Engineering
ESTCP	Facility-Related Control Systems Cybersecurity Guideline
UFC 4-010-01 Chg 1	DoD Minimum Antiterrorism Standards for Buildings
UFC 4-010-06	Cybersecurity of Facility-Related Control Systems
KGB Manual	SECRET KGB Manual for Recruitment of Spies (English)
FMFRP 3-201	Spetsnaz
C4ISR Facilities	C4ISR Facilities
DoD Law of War	2016 DoD Law of War Manual

Department of Defense
MANUAL

NUMBER 5205.07, Volume 1
June 18, 2015
Incorporating Change 1, Effective February 12, 2018

USD(I)

SUBJECT: DoD Special Access Program (SAP) Security Manual: General Procedures

References: See Enclosure 1

1. PURPOSE.

a. <u>Manual</u>. This manual is composed of several volumes, each containing its own purpose. The purpose of the overall manual, in accordance with the authority in DoD Directive (DoDD) 5143.01 (Reference (a)), is to implement policy established in DoDD 5205.07 (Reference (b)), assign responsibilities, and provide security procedures for DoD SAP information.

b. <u>Volume</u>. This volume:

(1) Assigns responsibilities, implements policy established in DoD Instruction (DoDI) 5205.11 (Reference (c)), and describes the general procedures for the administration of DoD SAP security.

(2) Incorporates and cancels Revision 1 Department of Defense Overprint to the National Industrial Security Program (NISP) Operating Manual Supplement (Reference (d)).

2. APPLICABILITY. This volume applies to:

a. OSD, the Military Departments, the Office of the Chairman of the Joint Chiefs of Staff and the Joint Staff, the Combatant Commands, the Office of the Inspector General of the Department of Defense, the Defense Agencies, the DoD Field Activities, and all other organizational entities within the DoD (referred to collectively in this volume as the "DoD Components").

b. All DoD Component contractors and consultants who require access to DoD SAPs pursuant to the terms and conditions of the contract or agreement.

c. Non-DoD U.S. Government (USG) departments, activities, agencies, and all other organizational entities that require access to DoD SAPs pursuant to the terms and conditions of a memorandum of agreement (MOA) or other interagency agreement established with the DoD.

3. <u>POLICY</u>. It is DoD policy according to Reference (b) that DoD SAPs be established and maintained when absolutely necessary to protect the most sensitive DoD capabilities, information, technologies, and operations or when required by statute.

4. <u>RESPONSIBILITIES</u>. See Enclosure 2.

5. <u>PROCEDURES</u>. Follow the procedures in Reference (b), those in Enclosures 3-12 of this volume, and the processing procedures and templates posted on the Defense Security Service (DSS) Website found at http://www.dss.mil/isp/specialprograms.html. Requests for clarification of this volume will be forwarded through the Program Security Officer to the cognizant authority (CA) SAP Central Office (SAPCO) for resolution. The SAPCO can contact the Office of the Under Secretary of Defense for Intelligence (USD(I)) for SAP security policy clarification as needed.

6. <u>RELEASABILITY</u>. **Cleared for public release**. ~~This volume is available on the Internet from the DoD Issuances Website at http://www.dtic.mil/whs/directives.~~ *This volume is available on the Directives Division Website at http://www.esd.whs.mil/DD/.*

7. <u>EFFECTIVE DATE</u>. This volume is effective June 18, 2015.

Marcel Lettre
Acting Under Secretary of Defense
for Intelligence

Enclosures
  1. References
  2. Responsibilities
  3. Functional Roles
  4. General Provisions and Requirements
  5. Safeguarding Classified Information
  6. Cybersecurity
  7. SETA Program
  8. Security Incidents and Inquiries
  9. SAP Compliance Inspections
  10. Visit Request Procedures
  11. Contracting
  12. SAP Technology Transfers
  13. Glossary

TABLE OF CONTENTS

ENCLOSURE 1

REFERENCES

(a) DoD Directive 5143.01, "Under Secretary of Defense for Intelligence (USD(I))," October 24, 2014, as amended
(b) DoD Directive 5205.07, "Special Access Program (SAP) Policy," July 1, 2010
(c) DoD Instruction 5205.11, "Management, Administration, and Oversight of DoD Special Access Programs (SAPs)", February 6, 2013
(d) Revision 1 Department of Defense Overprint to the National Industrial Security Program Operating Manual Supplement, April 1, 2004 (hereby cancelled)
(e) DoD Instruction 5220.22, "National Industrial Security Program (NISP)," March 18, 2011
(f) DoD 5220.22-R, "Industrial Security Regulation," December 4, 1985
(g) DoD 5220.22-M, "National Industrial Security Program Operating Manual," February 28, 2006, as amended
(h) DoD 8570.01-M, "Information Assurance Workforce Improvement Program," December 19, 2005, as amended
(i) DoD Directive 5000.01, "The Defense Acquisition System," May 12, 2003
(j) DoD Instruction 5000.02, "Operation of the Defense Acquisition System," January 7, 2015, *as amended*
(k) DoD Joint Special Access Program Implementation Guide (JSIG), October 9, 2013
(l) DoD Manual 5105.21 Volume 2, "Sensitive Compartmented Information (SCI) Administrative Security Manual: Administration of Physical Security, Visitor Control, and Technical Security" October 19, 2012
(m) DoD Directive 5205.02E, "DoD Operations Security (OPSEC) Program," June 20, 2012
(n) DoD Directive 2060.1, "Implementation of, and Compliance with, Arms Control Agreements," January 9, 2001
(o) DoD Directive 5240.02, "Counterintelligence," March 17, 2015
(p) DoD Instruction 5240.10, "Counterintelligence (CI) in the Combatant Commands and Other DoD Components," October 5, 2011, as amended
(q) National Policy and Procedures for the Disclosure of Classified Military Intelligence to Foreign Governments and International Organizations, short title: National Disclosure Policy-1 (NDP-1), October 1, 1988[1]
(r) DoD Directive 5230.11, "Disclosure of Classified Military Information to Foreign Governments and International Organizations," June 16, 1992
(s) DoD Directive 5530.3, "International Agreements," June 11, 1987, as amended
(t) Executive Order 13526, "Classified National Security Information," December 29, 2009
(u) DoD Manual 5200.01, Volume 3, "DoD Information Security Program: Protection of Classified Information," February 24, 2012, as amended
(v) Section 119 of Title 10, United States Code
(w) Part 2, Appendix D of Title 42, United States Code
(x) Committee on National Security Systems Policy (CNSSP) No. 22, "National Policy on Information Assurance Risk Management for National Security Systems," January, 2012

---

[1] Provided to designated disclosure authorities on a need-to-know basis from the Defense Technology Security Administration's International Security Directorate.

(y) Intelligence Community Directive Number 503, "Intelligence Community Information Technology Systems Security Risk Management, Certification and Accreditation," September 15, 2008

(z) Directive-type Memorandum 09-012, "Interim Policy Guidance for DoD Physical Access Control," December 8, 2009, as amended

(aa) DoD Manual 5220.22, Volume 3, "National Industrial Security Program: Procedures for Government Activities Relating to Foreign Ownership, Control, or Influence (FOCI)," April 17, 2014

(ab) Part 2004 of Title 32, Code of Federal Regulations

ENCLOSURE 2

RESPONSIBILITIES

1. <u>USD(I)</u>. The Office of the USD(I) is the office of primary responsibility for the development and maintenance of this volume.

2. <u>DIRECTOR, DSS</u>. Under the authority, direction, and control of the USD(I), the Director, DSS:

   a. Administers the NISP in accordance with DoDI 5220.22 (Reference (e)), DoD 5220.22-R (Reference (f)), and DoD 5220.22-M (Reference (g)).

   b. Issues facility security clearances (FCLs) for defense contractors performing on all DoD classified contracts, to include contractors performing on DoD SAPs.

   c. Unless a carve-out provision is approved by the Secretary of Defense or the Deputy Secretary of Defense:

      (1) Performs SAP security inspections at cleared defense contractor locations in accordance with this volume, Reference (f), and the government contracting activity's completed DD Form 254, "Department of Defense Contract Security Classification Specification," located at http://www.dtic.mil/whs/directives/infomgt/forms/formsprogram.htm.

      (2) Authorizes classified contractor SAP information systems (ISs) and the introduction of guest systems in contractor SAP facilities (SAPFs).

      (3) Coordinates with the designated counterintelligence (CI) component to provide cross-sharing of threat and incident information affecting the security of the facility or its defense information or cleared personnel.

   d. Maintains and trains a cadre of personnel proficient in policies, procedures, and security, as codified in this manual.

3. <u>DIRECTOR, DoD SAPCO</u>. Under the authority, direction, and control of the Deputy Secretary of Defense, the Director, DoD SAPCO:

   a. Serves as the DoD designated proponent for developing and implementing policies and procedures for DoD SAP execution, management, and administration.

   b. Functions as the DoD single point of Congressional liaison concerning SAPs.

   c. Supports departmental efforts to resolve issues and decisions related to SAP security, technology transfer, technology export, the Committee on Foreign Investment in the United

States, mutual participation by foreign partners, bilateral collaboration, and foreign ownership, control, and influence (FOCI).

4. <u>DoD CIO</u>. In coordination with the Director, DoD SAPCO, the DoD CIO:

    a. Establishes and administers governance and risk management policies to develop enterprise SAP information technology (IT) strategy, telecommunications infrastructure policy, SAP network IT requirements, and network and systems funding oversight policy in accordance with Reference (c).

    b. Develops and issues supplemental policies and procedures for cybersecurity and authorization of DoD SAP ISs.

    c. Establishes requirements and participation parameters for secure networks, databases, and ISs that support SAP governance and reciprocity within the DoD SAP communities.

5. <u>DoD COMPONENT HEADS AND OSD PRINCIPAL STAFF ASSISTANTS (PSAs) WITH CA AND OVERSIGHT AUTHORITY (OA) OVER SAPS</u>. The DoD Component heads and the OSD PSAs with CA and OA over SAPs:

    a. Identify an inspection official responsible for implementing a SAP compliance inspection program in accordance with Enclosure 9 of this volume.

    b. Comply with DoD 8570.01-M (Reference (h)) for IA training requirements.

    c. Coordinate with the DSS CI Directorate to provide cross-sharing of threat and incident information affecting the security of the facility or its defense information or cleared personnel and cleared contractors under the NISP when the SAP is carved out of DSS oversight.

6. <u>DIRECTORS OF THE DoD COMPONENT SAPCOs AND DIRECTORS OF THE PSAs SAPCOs WITH CA AND OA OVER SAPs</u>. Under the authority, direction, and control of their respective DoD Component heads and PSAs, the Directors of the DoD Component SAPCOs and the PSA SAPCOs with CA and OA over SAPs:

    a. Develop policies and procedures for the implementation of the requirements of this volume within their respective component, as required.

    b. Oversee, establish, and manage continuing security awareness training and program requirements to ensure complete, common, and continuing application of SAP security.

    c. Establish a SAP Information Security program, defining SAP accountability requirements.

    d. Provide support and oversight of their SAP IS security program.

e. Plan and budget for cybersecurity resources for SAPs under their purview.

ENCLOSURE 3

FUNCTIONAL ROLES

1. <u>GOVERNMENT PROGRAM MANAGER (GPM)</u>. The GPM:

    a. Manages designated SAPs.

    b. Implements and executes SAP security countermeasures in accordance with all applicable laws; national, DoD, and DoD Component issuances relating to or governing DoD SAPs; and this volume.

    c. Monitors and assigns personnel, financial resources, and facilities required to establish, support, and maintain SAPs and security compliance.

    d. Implements operations security (OPSEC), treaty, and arms control measures needed to support the SAP and ensure a tailored Security Education and Training Awareness (SETA) program for all briefed personnel.

    e. Plans and budgets for program cybersecurity resources, ensuring compliance with established cybersecurity policy for all systems, including those under contract or vendor-provided.

    f. Complies with applicable cybersecurity and technology acquisition requirements in accordance with DoDD 5000.01 (Reference (i)) and Interim DoDI 5000.02 (Reference (j)) for all IS acquisitions.

    g. Serves as the IS Owner in accordance with the DoD Joint Special Access Program Implementation Guide (Reference (k)).

2. <u>PSO</u>. The PSO, appointed by the CA SAPCO, is responsible for the program security management and execution of all security policies and requirements for a specific SAP(s) program(s), compartment(s), sub-compartment(s), or project(s), and:

    a. Works with the GPM to develop, implement, and enforce a security program that protects all facets of the SAP. Provides security subject matter expertise to the GPM and oversight to assigned programs to ensure compliance with all established policy and procedures.

    b. Provides oversight and direction for SETA programs.

    c. Provides oversight and direction to government SAP security officers (GSSOs) and contractor program security officers (CPSOs) designated to support SAPs.

d. Conducts or verifies that all approved SAPFs are properly inspected for security compliance.

e. In coordination with the appropriate government CI activity, applies risk management principles to SAP security architectures and environments for which the PSO is responsible. These principles include but are not limited to:

(1) Identify, characterize, and assess threats.

(2) Assess the vulnerability of critical assets to specific threats.

(3) Determine the risk (i.e., the expected likelihood and consequences of specific types of attacks on specific assets).

(4) Identify ways to mitigate those risks.

(5) Identify and assess cost and resources to mitigate those risks.

(6) Prioritize risk mitigation measures based on a strategy.

f. Approves changes to the environment and operational needs that could affect the security authorization in accordance with Reference (k).

g. Verifies that configuration management policies and procedures for authorizing the use of hardware and software on an IS are followed in accordance with Reference (k).

h. Ensures that each assigned GSSO and CPSO conducts and documents annual self-inspection. Approves the resultant corrective actions to establish or ensure compliance.

i. Ensures that a SAP trained and knowledgeable GSSO or CPSO, as appropriate, is assigned to serve as the SAP security official at each organization or facility.

j. Initiates and directs security investigations and inquiries to fully explore and document security incidents.

3. <u>GSSOs and CPSOs</u>. GSSOs and CPSOs:

a. Coordinate with the PSO and the GPM or Contractor Program Manager (CPM), respectively, to create a secure environment to facilitate the successful development and execution of a SAP(s) at each organization or location where SAP information is stored, accessed, or SAP-accessed personnel are assigned.

b. Are responsible for security management, to include SETA, and operations within their assigned activity, organization, or office.

1-13

c. Adhere to applicable laws as well as national, DoD, and other security SAP policies and requirements.

d. Coordinate SAP security matters with the PSO and GPM or CPM, respectively.

e. Establish, conduct, and document initial, event-driven, and annual refresher training for all assigned SAP-accessed individuals.

f. Conduct an annual self-inspection, document the self-inspection, and submit to the PSO a corrective action plan that identifies actions to establish compliance.

4. <u>CPM</u>. CPMs will:

a. Assign in writing a CPSO to serve as the SAP security official at each contractor organization or location where SAP information is stored or accessed or SAP-accessed personnel are assigned.

b. Be responsible for execution for the statement of work, contract, task orders, and all other contractual obligations.

5. <u>TOP SECRET (TS) CONTROL OFFICER (TSCO)</u>. TSCOs will be responsible for the receipt, dispatch, transmission, and maintenance of access, accountability, and inventory records for TS SAP material. TSCOs will be designated in writing by the GPM or CPM, when the PSO determines a program requires a TSCO. The processes used by the TSCO will be thoroughly documented in the standard operating procedures (SOPs).

ENCLOSURE 4

GENERAL PROVISIONS AND REQUIREMENTS

1. SOP.

    a. The GSSO or CPSO will prepare SOPs to implement the security policies and requirements unique to their facilities and the SAP.

    b. The GSSO or CPSO will forward the proposed SOPs and SOP changes to the PSO, for approval.

    c. A SOP is not required for a pre-solicitation activity, a research and development announcement, a request for information, or a request for proposal when there is no contractual relationship established for that effort or when contractors perform SAP work at government facilities only and not at contractor facilities. In these instances, classification guidance and special security rules reflected on the DD Form 254 and in the Security Classification Guide (SCG) suffice as the SOP.

    d. Special security instructions will be instituted outlining the procedures that protect the information and are compliant with the security policy reflected on the DD Form 254 and expressly incorporated into the contract.

    e. A SOP template is posted on the DSS website at http://www.dss.mil/isp/specialprograms.html. At a minimum, the following topics will be addressed in the SOP:

        (1) General provision and requirements.

        (2) Reporting requirements.

        (3) Security clearances.

        (4) SETA program.

        (5) Classification and markings.

        (6) Safeguarding classified information.

        (7) Visits and meetings.

        (8) Subcontracting.

        (9) ISs.

2. REPORTING REQUIREMENTS. Reports required based on this volume are posted on the DSS website at http://www.dss.mil/isp/specialprograms.html. At a minimum, report the following to the PSO:

   a. Adverse Information

   b. Refusal to sign a SAP Indoctrination Agreement

   c. Change in Employee Status

   d. Employees Desiring Not to Perform on SAP Classified Work

   e. Foreign Travel

   f. Changes or modifications to the SAP area accreditation

3. FRAUD, WASTE, ABUSE, AND CORRUPTION (FWAC).

   a. Government and industry FWAC SAP reporting involving SAP information will be accomplished through SAP channels. Collateral FWAC reporting channels must not be used for SAP information.

   b. The PSO will provide the telephone number for the current FWAC hotline for reporting SAP information. FWAC reporting information will be conspicuously posted in the SAP workspace.

   c. Employees do not need management approval before making reports.

4. CO-UTILIZATION AGREEMENT (CUA). The CUA documents areas of authorities and responsibilities between cognizant security offices (CSOs) when they share the same SAPF. A CUA will be executed between CSOs. The first CSO in an area, unless otherwise agreed upon, will be considered the host CSO responsible for all security oversight. The CUA will be initiated by the tenant PSO and approved by all parties before introduction of the additional SAP(s) into the SAPF.

   a. Topics to be included in a CUA include: compliance inspection responsibility, incident notification, and host-tenant agreement to clarify inspection responsibilities. All CUAs will be reviewed and updated on a biannual basis.

   b. Agencies desiring to co-utilize a SAPF will accept the current accreditation of the cognizant agency. Prospective tenant activities will be informed of all waivers to the requirements of this manual before co-utilization. Any security enhancements required by an agency or department requesting co-utilization should be funded by that organization and must be approved by the appropriate CA SAPCO before implementation. Any changes to the approved CUA must be submitted to the appropriate PSOs before implementing the changes.

    c. For CUAs, the responsible organization will be identified for executing security cognizance with a carved-out SAP.

    d. Co-utilization of Sensitive Compartmented Information (SCI) within a SAPF, or SAP within an SCI facility, will require authorization from the PSO and the servicing special security officer in accordance with Volume 2 of DoD Manual (DoDM) 5105.21 (Reference (l)).

5. <u>OPSEC</u>. All SAPs will have an OPSEC program developed and maintained in accordance with DoDD 5205.02E (Reference (m)).

6. <u>PROGRAM PROTECTION PLAN (PPP)</u>. All SAPs will develop, implement, and maintain a PPP or alternative documents that, when combined, meet the intent of the PPP.

7. <u>PATENTS AND INTELLECTUAL PROPERTY</u>. The CA SAPCO will develop procedures for processing patents and intellectual property involving SAP(s).

8. <u>ARMS CONTROL AND TREATIES.</u>

    a. DoDD 2060.1 (Reference (n)) establishes the arms control implementation and compliance responsibilities for SAPs; in accordance with Reference (b), treaty compliance requirements, obligations, or constraints will be considered as an integral part of the policy. DoD SAPs must be prepared to comply with treaties and agreements to which the USG is a signatory. DoD SAPs will be protected against unnecessary or inadvertent exposure during USG participation in authorized verification activities, confidence-building measures, and over flights.

    b. The PSO, GSSO, and CPSO should be familiar with various arms control verification activities in order to exercise security oversight for SAPs. Arms control treaty guidance and procedures are located at the website http://www.dss.mil/isp/specialprograms.html.

9. <u>LITIGATION AND PUBLIC PROCEEDINGS.</u>

    a. Threatened or actual litigation, administrative investigations or inquiries, or public proceedings at the international, federal, State, tribal, or local levels that may involve a SAP will be reported to CA SAPCO. Appropriate DoD general counsel offices or judge advocate offices will be notified of potential litigation issues at the earliest possible time. These proceedings include legal or administrative actions in which the prime contractor, subcontractors, or government organizations and SAP-accessed individuals are a named party (plaintiff, defendant, or witness).

b. DoD government and contractor personnel accessed to DoD SAPs will inform the PSO of any litigation actions that may pertain to the SAP, to include litigation regarding the physical environments, facilities, or personnel, or as otherwise directed by the GPM. PSOs will be notified of employee or union strikes, employer discrimination complaints, Equal Employment Opportunity cases, Merit Service Protection Board appeals, litigation, etc. in accordance with the timelines required by Enclosure 2, paragraph 5.s of Reference (c).

10. <u>CI SUPPORT.</u>

a. Analysis of foreign intelligence threats and risks to SAP information, material, personnel, and activities will be undertaken in accordance with DoDD O-5240.02 (Reference (o)); by the organic CI organization or by the lead military department CI organization in accordance with DoDI 5240.10 (Reference (p)). Information that may have a bearing on the security of a SAP will be provided by the government or military CI agency to the affected SAP PM and PSO, as necessary.

b. Contractors may use CI support to enhance or assist security planning and safeguarding in pursuit of satisfying contractual obligations. Requests for SAP-applicable CI support will be made to the respective PSO before contractors receiving such support.

11. <u>COMMUNICATIONS SECURITY.</u> SAP information will be electronically transmitted by approved secure communications channels authorized by the SOP.

12. <u>INTERNATIONAL SAP SECURITY REQUIREMENTS.</u>

a. The National Disclosure Policy (NDP-1) (Reference (q)) governs all foreign disclosures of classified military information. Security planning for foreign disclosure is an ongoing process that requires reviews at each milestone in the SAP lifecycle.

(1) All SAPs will comply with Reference (q). SAPs will include foreign disclosure and security planning at the beginning of the prospective SAP process or at the earliest possible date foreign disclosure is identified in an ongoing SAP. When a SAP is identified for international cooperation or foreign disclosure, all foreign disclosure and policy guidance will be in accordance with Reference (q), DoDD 5230.11 (Reference (r)), and DoDD 5530.3 (Reference (s)).

(2) The foreign disclosure officer and CA SAPCO do not have authority to disclose SAPs without Secretary of Defense or Deputy Secretary of Defense approval, in accordance with Reference (b).

b. The GPM and PSO will coordinate with their Component Foreign Disclosure Office and CA SAPCO to develop technology assessment or control plans, MOAs, and security documentation for all international SAPs as appropriate. Additional security requirements are further identified in bilateral program-specific security agreements, General Security of Military Information Agreements, and Industrial Security Arrangements.

ENCLOSURE 5

SAFEGUARDING CLASSIFIED INFORMATION

1. <u>HANDLE VIA SPECIAL ACCESS CHANNELS ONLY (HVSACO)</u>.

   a. The purposes of HVSACO are:

   (1) To preclude the disclosure of general program-related information outside established acknowledged and unacknowledged SAP channels.

   (2) To minimize OPSEC indicators.

   (3) To facilitate communication of information within SAPs.

   b. Dissemination of information warranting HVSACO protection will be limited to persons briefed into a SAP and retained within SAP approved channels. Formal SAP indoctrination or execution of briefing or debriefing forms specifically for HVSACO is not required. The term SAP channels denote secure, approved SAP communications systems, SAPFs, or PSO-approved SAP storage areas. HVSACO is not a classification level, but rather a protection or handling system. Examples of HVSACO uses may include:

   (1) For general non-program specific communications between and within SAPs. More specifically, on information related to SAP security procedures, test plans, transportation plans, manufacturing plans, and notional concepts related to research, development, testing, and evaluation of SAPs.

   (2) When a paragraph or document contains information that is unique to a SAP and its distribution.

   (3) When necessary to protect sensitive relationships.

   (4) To protect information that does not warrant classification under Executive Order 13526 (Reference (t)).

   (5) When using a SAP nickname for an unacknowledged SAP.

   c. Upon request for public release, the originator of the material must review the material involved to determine whether to retain it within program channels:

   (1) If public release is appropriate, remove the HVSACO marking from the document; or

   (2) Inform the requestor of the decision not to release the information, citing an appropriate authority.

d. Training on HVSACO should be included in annual security awareness refresher sessions.

e. Procedures for the use of HVSACO should be included in Program SCGs.

f. Materials warranting HVSACO protection must be stored in accordance with the SOP. Unclassified HVSACO materials may be stored openly within an approved SAPF taking into account OPSEC considerations. PSOs may grant an exception to allow the taking of unclassified HVSACO materials to alternate temporary storage areas, provided the material is under an appropriately authorized individual's direct control, or under "key lock protection" which is controlled by that individual.

g. Transmission of SAP material.

(1) At a minimum, use U.S. First Class mail for shipment of unclassified materials requiring HVSACO protection.

(2) Use the secure mode when discussing HVSACO-protected material on authorized telephones.

(3) Use only approved, secure facsimile (FAX) equipment when transmitting HVSACO-protected material.

(4) Do not transmit HVSACO-protected material via unclassified e-mail.

h. Reproduce unclassified HVSACO-protected information only on equipment approved by the PSO.

i. HVSACO protection does not require accountability. Document accountability is based on classification level or unique program requirements. Document control numbers, entry into document control systems, or internal or external receipts are not required for unclassified HVSACO-protected material.

j. Destroy HVSACO-protected information according to the procedures approved for classified material. Destruction certificates are not required for non-accountable HVSACO-protected materials.

k. Based on an assessment of the OPSEC risk, notify the PSO within 24 hours of any possible improper handling or misuse of HVSACO-protected information and its impact. An inquiry should be conducted to determine if a compromise occurred as a result of practices dangerous to security. The PSO will ensure that prompt corrective action is taken on any practices dangerous to security.

l. Contact the originating office for permission to remove HVSACO markings.

2. USE OF SECURE ENCRYPTION DEVICES AND ELECTRONIC TRANSMISSION EQUIPMENT.

a. Secure Encryption Devices.

(1) SAP government and industry organizations must use National Security Agency/Central Security Service (NSA/CSS) approved or certified Type I encrypted secure communications for the electronic transmission of all classified information.

(2) All products used for the electrical transmission of classified or sensitive information must be used in accordance with prescribed national and associated policies or doctrine.

b. Secure FAX. Secure FAX encrypted communications equipment may be used for the transmission of SAP information. When secure FAX is permitted, the PSO will approve the system in writing.

(1) Do not use FAX terminals equipped with the automatic polling function enabled unless authorized by the PSO.

(2) When approved by the PSO, SAP documents classified SECRET (S) SAP and below may be receipted via an automated generated message that confirms undisturbed transmission and receipt. A transmission log will be maintained and validated during GSSO or CPSO self-inspections and made available for review during inspections.

(3) When transmitting TS SAP documents over a secure FAX terminal, the recipient must acknowledge receipt of the TS SAP material. The recipient will return a signed receipt after completion of transmission. The transmission and receipt of TS material will be recorded by the sender in a FAX log.

c. Electronic Transmission. When using electronic transmission (e.g., voice over internet protocol, video teleconferencing for SAP material), encrypted communications equipment will be used. When secure electronic transmission is permitted, the authorizing official, in coordination with the PSO, will approve the system in writing to the GSSO or CPSO.

3. CONTROL.
SAP classified material, hardware, equipment and all media not subject to accountability will be controlled by the procedures implemented by policy, training, and awareness that:

a. Regulate and monitor the introduction and exit of all controlled items from all SAPFs.

b. Identify and document:

(1) The identity of the custodian, date created (or entered the SAPFs) and date destroyed (or exited the SAPFs).

(2) Classification, Program sensitivity (e.g. TS, S//SAR-XYZ, U//HVSACO, For Official Use Only (FOUO), Unclassified (U), personally identifiable information).

(3) Type (e.g. documents, hard disks, compact disks, universal serial bus storage devices).

(4) Content (e.g., application software, non-writable or writable, engineering notebook).

c. At least on an annual basis, the continued need for all controlled items will be assessed and items no longer required will be destroyed.

d. Safeguarding of classified information, to include SAP material, will be done in accordance with Volume 3 of DoDM 5200.01 (Reference (u)), unless otherwise noted in this volume.

4. ACCOUNTABILITY.

a. An accountability system approved by the PSO will be developed and maintained for the following SAP classified information.

(1) All TS SAP material, media, hardware, equipment, etc.

(2) S SAP material, media, hardware, equipment, etc. when directed by the CA SAPCO.

(3) All other classified media when directed by the CA SAPCO.

b. Accountable SAP material will be entered into an accountability system whenever it is received, generated, reproduced, or dispatched either internally or externally to other SAPFs. The accountability system will be designed to record all transactions of handling, receipt, generation, reproduction, dispatch, or destruction. The accountability system will assign individual responsibility for all accountable information. An automated system, if used, will have a backup. When SAP material is received with the originator's accountability control number, the accountability system will include the originator's accountability control number.

c. The accountability system will have at the minimum:

(1) Classification.

(2) Originator of the item.

(3) Title and description of item.

(4) Custodian assigned.

(5) Date of product.

(6) Control number (maintained in consecutive number series).

(7) Copy number.

(8) Page count.

(9) Disposition and date.

(10) Destruction date.

(11) Internal and external receipt records

d. A disclosure sheet will be maintained for each TS item. The name is recorded only once regardless of the number of times subsequent access occurs. Once destruction of a TS product takes place, the TS access record will be kept with the destruction paperwork and destroyed 3 years after the document is destroyed.

e. Electronic files do not need to be placed into accountability systems or the information management system referenced in paragraph 4a of this enclosure when residing on ISs or receipted when transmitted between system users within the same unified network provided the data remains resident within the IS.

5. <u>ANNUAL INVENTORY.</u>

a. A 100 percent inventory of accountable SAP material will be conducted annually by the individual responsible for the control system or their alternate and a disinterested party. The annual inventory date will not exceed the previous year's inventory date by more than 12 months. Inventories will be conducted by visual inspection of all items of accountable SAP material and verification of pertinent information (originator, date, subject, file number, etc.) and page count for TS SAP held within the SAPF.

b. Inventories of TS material will be documented by the TSCO and a second disinterested individual and made available during security compliance inspections. Discrepancies will be reported immediately to the PSO, who will ensure action is taken, as appropriate, in accordance with Enclosure 8 of this volume.

6. <u>COLLATERAL CLASSIFIED MATERIAL.</u>

a. The PSO will provide oversight for collateral classified material maintained in the SAP. The process for introduction of collateral material will be approved by the PSO. Collateral material assigned or produced under a collateral contract required to support a SAP will be PSO-approved before the introduction, inclusion, or production, and may be transferred within SAP controls.

b. Transfer will be accomplished in a manner that will not compromise the SAP or any classified information. Collateral classified material generated during the performance of a SAP contract may be transferred from the SAP to another SAP or collateral program.

7. <u>TRANSMISSION AND PREPARATION OF SAP CLASSIFIED MATERIAL.</u>

a. SAP information will only be transmitted outside the SAPF using one of the methods identified within this section. The GSSO or CPSO will oversee transmission of SAP material. The order of precedence for transmission processes is:

(1) Cryptographic communications systems (i.e., secure facsimile, IS).

(2) Courier.

(3) PSO approved government or commercial carrier for S SAP material and below.

(4) Defense Courier Service for TS SAP material.

(5) United States Postal Service (USPS) registered mail or US Express Mail for S SAP material and below within the continental United States (CONUS).

(6) USPS certified mail for <u>CONFIDENTIAL</u> SAP material and below within CONUS.

b. SAP material being mailed or couriered will be prepared, reproduced, and packaged by the appropriately cleared SAP-briefed personnel inside the SAPF.

(1) Dispatch receipts are required for the transmission of SAP material.

(2) Classify receipts according to content.

(3) Inner and outer wrapping markings.

(a) Inner wrappings will be opaque and marked with the "TO" and "FROM" blocks and will bear the highest level of classification marking of the content.

(b) Outer wrappings will be opaque and will show an unclassified address on the "TO" and "FROM" blocks.

(4) When a receipt is not returned within 15 days, contact the recipient to determine status of the material. If the material is received, have the recipient provide the receipt. If the recipient did not receive the material, immediately initiate a preliminary inquiry and inform the PSO and the GPM.

c. SAP material will be transported from one SAPF to another in an unobtrusive and secure manner.

(1) Courier(s) must be accessed to the level of SAP being couriered.

(2) For local travel, SAP material may be hand-carried using a locked container as the outer wrapper. Local travel will be defined by CA SAPCO. Travel outside of the defined local area of the originating SAPF requires PSO approval. Attach a tag or label with the individual's name, organization, and telephone number.

(3) Travel should be performed using a personal, company owned, rented, or government vehicle. Use of public transportation requires PSO approval.

(4) TS SAP working papers taken to another SAPF in the same building for collaboration that will be returned before the expiration of the working paper time limits does not need to be placed into accountability when leaving the SAPF. Hand receipts documenting item and page count are still required.

d. When approved by the PSO, a USPS mailing channel may be established to ensure mail is received only by appropriately cleared and accessed personnel. Use USPS-registered mail or USPS Express Mail for S SAP material. Use USPS certified mail for CONFIDENTIAL SAP. "For Official Use Only" and unclassified HVSACO, material may be sent by First Class mail. When associations present an OPSEC concern in receiving and sending mail, the GSSO or CPSO will establish and use a sterile Post Office box with the written approval from the PSO.

(1) Except for TS SAP material, a USG-approved contract carrier (i.e., USPS Express Mail) can be used for overnight transmission on a case-by-case basis with approval of the PSO. Packages may only be shipped on Monday through Thursday and delivery date must be checked to ensure that the carrier does not retain the classified package over a holiday or weekend.

(2) These methods of transmitting selected SAP information are in addition to, not a replacement for, other transmission means previously approved for such material. Use of secure electronic means is the preferred method of transmission.

(3) Except for approved USPS means, use overnight delivery only when:

(a) Written approval is received by the PSO.

(b) SAP requirements dictate.

(c) Essential to mission accomplishment.

(d) Time is of the essence, negating other approved methods of transmission.

(e) Receiver of material will be readily available to sign upon arrival.

(4) To ensure direct delivery to address provided by the PSO:

(a) Do not execute the waiver of signature and indemnity on USPS label.

(b) Do not execute the release portion on commercial carrier forms.

(c) Ensure an appropriate recipient is designated and available to receive material.

(d) Do not disclose to the express service carrier that the package contains classified material.

(5) Immediately report any problem, misplaced, or non-delivery, loss, or other security incident encountered with this transmission means to the PSO.

e. The GSSO or CPSO will provide detailed courier instructions and training to SAP-briefed couriers when hand-carrying SAP information. Problems encountered will be immediately reported to the PSO, who may authorize exceptions when operational considerations or emergency situations dictate. The following rules will be adhered to when couriering classified material:

(1) The responsible PSO is required to approve all couriering of TS SAP material. Two-person courier teams are required for all TS SAP material unless a single courier is authorized in writing by the PSO. The courier must be accessed to the level of SAP information being couriered.

(2) A single-person courier may be used for S SAP and below materials.

(3) Provisions will be made for additional couriers and overnight storage, when required (regardless of classification), when it appears continuous vigilance over the material cannot be sustained by a single individual.

(4) As a minimum, the GSSO or CPSO from the departure location will provide each authorized courier with a copy of Department of Defense (DD) Form 2501, "Courier Authorization," based on instructions located at http://www.dtic.mil/whs/directives/infomgt/forms/forminfo/forminfopage1828.html or a PSO approved locally produced courier authorization memorandum.

(a) At a minimum, the courier authorization and instructions will address:

1. Method of transportation.

2. Travel itinerary (intermittent or unscheduled stops, remain-overnight scenario), specific courier responsibilities (primary or alternate roles, as necessary).

3. Completion of receipts, as necessary, and full identification of the classified data being transferred.

<u>4</u>. A discussion of emergency or contingency plans (include after-hours points of contact, primary or alternate contact data, telephone numbers).

<u>5</u>. Each courier will acknowledge receipt and understanding of this briefing in writing.

(b) Experienced SAP-briefed individuals who frequently or routinely perform duties as classified couriers may be issued courier authorization cards or DD Form 2501 by the GSSO or CPSO in lieu of individual letters for each trip. The form is issued for no more than 1 year at a time. The requirement for authorization to hand carry will be revalidated on at least an annual basis and a new form issued, if appropriate.

8. <u>AIRPORT-SCREENING GUIDELINES FOR HANDLING CLASSIFIED MATERIAL.</u>

a. Travel to and from locations in the U.S. aboard commercial or government carriers.

(1) PSOs will apprise couriers of the limitations and restrictions surrounding screening procedures. Notifying government screening officials of courier status is not required until screening officials request to inspect classified material.

(2) When screening officials request to inspect classified material, couriers will:

(a) Allow the classified material to undergo the x-ray examination.

(b) Divest any material that may trigger the automated screening equipment.

(c) Place all metal objects and electronics on the x-ray belt or in a second bag.

(d) If the screening official desires to inspect the package after x-ray screening, the courier will:

<u>1</u>. Present the courier authorization letter and their government-issued identification.

<u>2</u>. Request assistance from the screening official's supervisor.

<u>3</u>. Request a private screening.

<u>4</u>. Permit the supervisor to inspect the outer package but not the contents. If the screening supervisor cannot determine if the material is cleared for transport, the courier will contact the originating PSO for further instructions.

b. Travel to or from locations outside the United States. Classified information will be sent via secure classified networks, classified FAX, or diplomatic pouch whenever possible. Hand-carrying SAP material other than by diplomatic courier should be used only as a last resort. Couriering classified SAP material on commercial aircraft is only approved by waiver issued by the Director, CA SAPCO, or designee.

c. Transportation Security Administration (TSA) Guidelines. The TSA publishes airport screening guidelines for handling classified material. GSSOs and CPSOs will ensure couriers are aware of the limitations and restrictions surrounding screening procedures.

9. <u>TRANSPORTATION PLANS</u>. The GSSO or CPSO will develop a transportation plan coordinated with and approved by the PSO at least 30 days in advance of the proposed movement. The transportation plan must:

a. Appoint a SAP-accessed individual knowledgeable about SAP security requirements to serve as the focal point for transportation issues.

b. Ensure that the planning includes priority of transportation modes (government surface, air, commercial surface, air) and inventory of classified SAP material to ensure SAP integrity.

c. Maintain a continuous chain of custody between the origination and destination, and comply with all Department of Transportation laws and SAP security requirements.

d. Include contingency planning (a description of emergency procedures, and who is responsible for actions that must be taken in the event of an emergency, e.g., unexpected stop anywhere along the route). Identify individuals by name, and provide their organization, telephone and fax numbers, and e-mail addresses.

e. Ensure CI support is incorporated into transportation planning and execution.

10. <u>RELEASE OF INFORMATION.</u>

a. Public release of SAP information is not authorized without written authority from the government in accordance with subtitle A, part 1, chapter 2, section 119 of Title 10 United States Code (U.S.C.) (Reference (v)) and part 2, appendix d of Title 42 U.S.C. (Reference (w)). Personnel are responsible to report any attempt by unauthorized personnel to obtain SAP information immediately to the PSO to the GPM.

(1) Information concerning SAPs must not be released to any non-SAP-accessed individual, firm, agency, or government activity without SAPCO approval. Classified or sensitive information concerning SAPs must not be included in general or unclassified publications, technical review documents, or marketing literature.

(2) All material proposed for release will be submitted through the PSO to the GPM 60 days before the proposed release date. After approval is granted, additional case-by-case requests to release identical data are not required.

b. Personnel currently or previously accessed to a SAP will provide the GPM and PSO with a copy of any proposed intended release of information that could potentially contain SAP information for review before public release. Information considered for release such as models, software, and technology that may impact other SAPs will require additional coordination with the DoD SAPCO, and other Component SAPCOs before release. The information and materials proposed for release will remain within SAP security channels until authorized for release.

c. The Defense Technical Information Center or the U.S. Department of Energy Office of Scientific and Technical Information does not accept SAP information.

d. Each SAP security officer will ensure the area SOP contains a process to ensure documents such as award nominations, performance reports, evaluations, etc. are reviewed to eliminate any program sensitive information before further dissemination.

11. <u>REPRODUCTION.</u>

a. SAP information will only be reproduced on equipment approved by the PSO. The GSSOs or CPSOs will prepare written reproduction procedures, and post a notice indicating if equipment can or cannot be used for reproduction of classified SAP material within a SAPF, and who is authorized to reproduce such material. Maintenance procedures will be written and incorporated into the SOPs listing the actions necessary when non-SAP briefed maintenance technicians' work on the equipment. When possible, an additional hard drive for maintenance purposes only should be purchased.

b. Equipment may be used outside a SAPF (e.g., within a SAP working area), provided written procedures are approved by the PSO which will include procedures for clearing of equipment, accessing of operators, clearing of media, handling malfunctions. GSSOs or CPSOs will position reproduction equipment to be continually monitored when it is outside a SAPF to achieve a risk mitigated solution. All reproduction equipment will be in compliance with applicable ISs guidance.

12. <u>DESTRUCTION.</u> Accountable SAP material will be destroyed using two SAP-briefed employees with access to the level of material being destroyed. Non-accountable SAP material may be destroyed by a single SAP-briefed employee with access to the level of material being destroyed. All classified waste containing SAP information will be destroyed as soon as possible. Such materials must not accumulate beyond 30 days unless approved by the PSO. NSA/CSS-approved equipment and their destruction procedures will be used to destroy SAP material as authorized by the PSO. Destruction of non-standard SAP materials will be approved by the PSO. Accountable and non-accountable SAP material will be maintained in accordance with the DoD Components record management manuals and instructions.

a. Prepare certificates of destruction itemizing each accountable document or material destroyed, to include citing the appropriate document control and copy number. For accountable

SAP material, destruction certificates must be completed and signed by both of the individuals involved in the destruction immediately after destruction is completed.

b. Public destruction facilities may be used only with the approval of and under conditions prescribed by the PSO.

ENCLOSURE 6

CYBERSECURITY

Reference (k) provides standardized cybersecurity related implementation guidance for policy and procedures for management of all networks, systems, and components at all classification levels for all DoD SAPs.

 a. All DoD SAP ISs that receive, process, store, display, or transmit SAP information must operate in compliance this manual and References (h) and (k).

 b. DoD SAP implementation of the Risk Management Framework, through the use of this manual, Annex B of Committee on National Security Systems Policy No. 22 (Reference (x)) and Reference (k) and in accordance with References (b) and (c), is aligned with Intelligence Community Directive Number 503 (Reference (y)).

 c. Additional or compensatory technical and non-technical countermeasures may, after consultation with the Director of the CA SAPCO or designee, be imposed in the interest of SAP protection in coordination with the PSO.

ENCLOSURE 7

SETA PROGRAM

1. <u>GENERAL</u>. GSSOs or CPSOs will ensure that the SETA program meets the specific and unique requirements of this manual. The SETA program applies to all SAP-accessed individuals. General, non-SAP specific, or company-wide security briefings may be used to form the basis for or supplement the SAP SETA requirement. Training on the unique, SAP, and SAPF specific parameters of the SAP is required.

2. <u>PSOs</u>. PSOs will approve the SETA program of assigned SAPs. This may be a standalone document or incorporated into the SAPF's SOP.

3. <u>GSSO(s) AND CPSO(s)</u>. GSSO(s) and CPSO(s) will:

   a. Establish a SETA program for their SAP(s).

   b. Annotate compliance with SETA requirements in the annual self-assessment checklist and provide to the responsible PSO in accordance with this volume.

4. <u>ANNUAL TRAINING</u>.

   a. Activities that grant SAP access will ensure that accessed individuals receive annual training to reaffirm their responsibilities while accessed to a SAP. When major changes occur such as changes in the classification for information protected under a SAP, new SAP-specific information that requires protection will be updated in briefings and training.

   b. Annual training by the PSO, GSSO, CPSO, or designee may take several different forms, to include but not limited to face-to-face briefings, computer-based presentations sent via e-mail on the appropriate classified network, single page data sheets requiring individual review and signature, or other methods as approved by the PSO.

      (1) Annual training will be recorded by utilizing the SAP training record template posted on the DSS website at http://www.dss.mil/isp/specialprograms.html.

      (2) If multiple SAPs are involved, a centralized record system may be utilized as approved by the PSO.

   c. SAP-accessed individuals will be briefed by PSOs, GSSOs, and CPSOs on individual reporting requirements during initial briefings and during annual training in accordance with this manual.

ENCLOSURE 8

SECURITY INCIDENTS AND INQUIRIES

To ensure the protection of classified information to include classified information protected by SAPs, security incidents will be investigated and actions will be taken to ensure that the adverse effects of loss or compromise of classified information are mitigated. Security incidents involving classified information will be handled and investigated in accordance with this manual and References (b) and (u).

a. All security violations will be reported immediately, to the extent possible, and no later than 24 hours of discovery, to the PSO, through the procedures described in this enclosure.

b. The PSO, through the chain of command, will advise the CA SAPCO in all instances where national security concerns would impact any security program or personnel security clearances (PCL) of SAP-accessed individuals. The PSO will notify and report security violations to the GPM with a copy of the report to the appropriate CA SAPCO. The security official of the affected SAPF will recommend the scope of the corrective action taken in response to the violation and report it to the PSO for approval.

c. Actual or potential compromises involving DoD SAPs, the results of the compromise or inquiries, and investigations that indicate weaknesses or vulnerabilities in establishing SAP policy, or procedures that contributed to an actual or potential compromise will be reported to the CA SAPCO, Original Classification Authority, and the DoD SAPCO, who will report to the Director of Security Policy and Oversight, Office of the USD(I).

d. Personnel determined to have had unauthorized or inadvertent access to classified SAP information:

    (1) Will be interviewed by the GSSO, CPSO, or PSO to determine the extent of the exposure.

    (2) May be requested to complete an inadvertent disclosure statement. An inquiry will be conducted to determine the circumstances of the inadvertent disclosure.

e. Guard personnel or local emergency authorities (e.g., police, medical, fire) inadvertently exposed to SAP material during an emergency response situation will be interviewed by the GSSO, CPSO, or PSO to determine the extent of the exposure.

    (1) The PSO will determine if an inquiry is required by Reference (u) to determine whether or not there was a loss of classified information or whether or not unauthorized personnel had, or could have had, access to the information.

(2) The inquiry identifies the facts, characterizes the incident as an infraction or a violation, and identifies, if possible, the cause(s) and person(s) responsible, reports corrective action or a requirement for an investigation.

f. Refusal to sign an inadvertent disclosure statement by personnel inadvertently exposed to classified information will be reported by the GSSO or CPSO to the PSO by the next duty day.

ENCLOSURE 9

SAP COMPLIANCE INSPECTIONS

1. GENERAL. The SAP security compliance process represents a unified and streamlined approach to the SAP security compliance inspections. All SAPs will be subject to the security compliance inspection process. The detailed guidance, procedures, and Security Inspection Checklist for conducting security compliance inspections are posted on the website http://www.dss.mil/isp/specialprograms.html.

2. INSPECTION TYPES. Inspections are conducted to validate that SAP security processes and procedures are in compliance with the governing DoD policies and to ensure that the risk of compromise to SAP information is at a minimum. Inspections should be executed with the least amount of impact to the SAP, while maintaining a proficient, equitable, and comprehensive review.

   a. There are four possible types of external inspections that can be conducted.

   (1) Core compliance inspections will be conducted at the direction of the inspection official, at a minimum every 2 years. The core compliance inspection consists of:

      (a) Self-inspection checklist

      (b) Core functional areas (CFAs)

         1. TS SAP data and materials accountability

         2. SETA

         3. Personnel security

         4. Security management and oversight

         5. Cybersecurity

         6. Physical security

      (c) Special emphasis items (SEIs)

   (2) Full scope inspections require a 100 percent validation of all functional areas. A full scope inspection will be conducted at the direction of the CA SAPCO when a less than satisfactory overall rating has been received as a result of a core compliance inspection. The most serious security rating, an unsatisfactory rating, is assigned when circumstances and conditions indicate that the program management personnel within the SAPF have lost, or are in

danger of losing, their ability to adequately safeguard the classified material in their possession or to which they have access.

(3) Re-inspections are required when a less than satisfactory rating in one or more functional areas has been received. This can include just one or all functional area(s), SAP(s), or SEI(s). The re-inspection will be conducted no later than 90 days from the issuance of the final report.

(4) Unannounced or No Notice inspections can be full-scope or core compliance inspections conducted without notice and at the discretion of the CA SAPCO or designee.

b. A security representative from the prime contractor should be present and participate during inspections of subcontractors. Designated personnel will serve as inspection team chiefs, assign ratings, conduct in or out briefings, or be responsible for completing the security inspection report.

c. Inspections will be coordinated among the SAPCOs and DSS when not carved out and conducted jointly to the greatest extent possible. Compliance inspections involving multiple SAP organizations will be fully coordinated between participating DoD organizations by the assigned team chiefs. Each organization is responsible for publishing its report.

3. SELF-INSPECTION. Self-inspections are required to be conducted annually by the GSSO, CPSO or designee, for all SAPFs for which they are assigned responsibility. Utilize the security compliance inspection template and document any deficiencies in a corrective action plan that addresses the plan for correcting deficiencies and areas deemed unsatisfactory as noted in the report. All supporting information will be included in the self-inspection report.

a. The documented results of self-inspections will be retained until the next government inspection is completed. All outstanding items must be completed before the destruction of any compliance documentation.

b. The documented results of the self-inspections will be submitted to the PSO for coordination within 30 days of completion. The PSO will be notified immediately if the self-inspection discloses the loss, compromise, or suspected compromise of SAP information.

c. In addition to the CFAs, inspectors will be required to validate SEIs. The CA SAPCO will annually determine the SEIs and report to the DoD SAPCO. The CA SAPCO will provide input on the trends and recommendations of the prior year to the DoD SAPCO.

4. STAFF ASSISTANCE VISIT (SAV). During a SAV, the PSO or designee will review security documentation and provide assistance and direction as necessary.

a. SAVs should be conducted as required and may include:

(1) Self-inspection checklists and corrective action plans.

(2) Outstanding government action items.

(3) Administrative security documentation (i.e., SOP, CPSO and IA manager appointment letter, OPSEC plan).

(4) Violations and infractions.

(5) SAP-specific CI trends and briefings.

(6) SETA program.

(7) Physical security standards.

(8) Cybersecurity.

(9) TS accountability.

b. The PSO will provide a SAV report to the GSSO or CPSO detailing what was covered and identifying all actions requiring resolution. During this visit, the PSO will provide guidance and direction to the organization, which will assist in the development of an effective and standardized security program. The PSO will annotate and address any concerns that require follow up before the next inspection.

5. <u>DEFICIENCIES</u>. Once the inspection has been completed, the team chief will determine the rating of the inspection based on the number of deficiencies identified and the risk of a compromise to classified information. Deficiencies will be defined as a finding or deviation.

6. <u>RATINGS</u>. Inspection ratings are superior, commendable, satisfactory, marginal, and unsatisfactory.

a. If the rating is superior, commendable, or satisfactory, the inspection official will discuss any deficiencies that may have been identified and provide the final inspection results in the SAP review report within 30 days and place the organization on an inspection cycle not to exceed 24 months.

b. If the rating is marginal, the inspection official will discuss any deficiencies that may have been identified and provide the final inspection results in the SAP review report within 30 days and schedule a re-inspection on the marginal areas within 90 days.

c. If the rating is unsatisfactory, the inspection official will discuss any deficiencies that may have been identified and provide the final inspection results in the SAP review report within 10 days and schedule a compliance security review to be conducted within 90 days.

ENCLOSURE 10

VISIT REQUEST PROCEDURES

1. GENERAL. Approval by the appropriate GPM or designated representative is required for all visits to SAP activities except for visits between the sites of a prime contractor and the prime's subcontractors, which may be approved by the CPM, or designee. A written or electronic visit notification must be approved before visiting a SAPF. Centralized personnel security databases may be used for access verification if authorized in writing by the responsible PSO or CA SAPCO, however GPM or designated representative approval of the visit is still required. All visit requests will be transmitted via PSO-approved channels.

2. ADVANCED NOTICE. SAP accessed personnel must make every effort to provide advance notification of the visit to their GSSO or CPSO. Visitors who courier classified material will provide travel itinerary, storage requirements, and emergency contact information to their GSSO or CPSO and the destination GSSO or CPSO.

3. UNANNOUNCED AND NON-VALIDATED ARRIVALS. Access will be denied if a visitor arrives at a government or contractor SAPF without verification of the requisite SAP accesses, except for the PSOs and supporting security staff members (as designated by the PSO) who may visit all SAPFs under their responsibility without furnishing advanced notification.

4. DURATION. Visit request authorizations in excess of 12 months are not permitted unless approved in writing by the PSO.

5. VALIDATION OF VISITOR'S IDENTIFICATION. The positive identification of each visitor will be made using an authorized credential in accordance with Directive-type Memorandum (DTM) 09-012 (Reference (z)); the identification number of the credential to be used will be annotated on the visit request. Federal Government-affiliated identification cards will not be used for positive identification in unacknowledged locations.

6. ESCORTING OF VISITORS.

    a. Only resident SAP-accessed personnel can escort and closely control movement of non-SAP accessed visitors requiring access to a SAPF. The number of escorts required will be dependent upon the number of visitors and the capability of closely monitoring the visitor activities.

    b. Foreign nationals visiting a SAPF will be approved by the CA SAPCO or designee.

c. The PSO or designee will determine whether an internal warning system (such as rotating light beacons) is necessary to warn accessed occupants of the presence of non-briefed personnel. The PSO or designee will employ other or additional methods (e.g., verbal announcements), as required, to warn or remind personnel of the presence of non-briefed personnel.

7. <u>TERMINATION OR CANCELLATION OF A VISIT REQUEST</u>. If a person is debriefed from the SAP before expiration of a visit request authorization, or if cancellation of a current visit request authorization is otherwise appropriate, the security officer or their designated representative will immediately notify all recipients of the cancellation or termination of the visit request authorization.

8. <u>VISITOR RECORDS</u>. Unless a PSO approved electronic visitor record is on file, the security officer will maintain segregated visitor logs for non-briefed and SAP accessed personnel. The visitor record will contain the visitor's:

   a. First and last name.

   b. Organization or firm.

   c. Date visited.

   d. Time in and out.

   e. Sponsor.

   f. Identification number of authorized credential in accordance with Reference (z).

   g. Citizenship.

   h. Purpose.

9. <u>CONGRESSIONAL VISITS</u>. The CA SAPCO will provide guidance when a congressional visit to a SAPF is proposed. In the event of the unannounced arrival of a congressional delegation, DoD employees accessed to DoD SAPs will contact the PSO for guidance. The PSO will contact the CA SAPCO for instructions. All communications and information flow between the authorized congressional members or their staff will be coordinated through the DoD SAPCO and CA SAPCO.

10. <u>UNFORESEEN OPERATIONAL OR EMERGENCY SITUATIONS</u>. When unforeseen events prevent providing a written or electronic visit notification, visit approval may be provided telephonically by the PSO or designee. Written certification and confirmation will follow verbal authorization within 24 hours.

ENCLOSURE 11

CONTRACTING

1. <u>CONTRACT SECURITY CLASSIFICATION SPECIFICATION (DD FORM 254)</u> <u>REQUIREMENTS</u>. The government contracting officer (GCO) awards contracts on behalf of the government and coordinates security requirements with the PSO. The PSO or designee prepares the DD Form 254. The GCO or designee signs as the certifying official for each prime contract. For subcontracts, the prime CPSO or designee prepares a DD Form 254 and forwards it to the PSO for review before release to subcontractors. Lengthy attachments to DD Form 254 that merely repeat information, policy, and procedures contained in any other security directives should not be included.

    a. SAP security guidelines, in addition to all collateral and SCI requirements, will be provided in the DD Form 254.

    b. The activity will notify the CA SAPCO if a government official imposes any security requirements exceeding those provided for in this manual. The activity will make the notification through the GCO who will generate a memorandum for signature by the CPM addressing the issues to the CA SAPCO.

2. <u>CLEARANCE STATUS OF SUBCONTRACTORS.</u> If a subcontractor does not have the requisite FCL, the prime CPSO or designee will submit a FCL request to DSS in accordance with Reference (e). Subcontractor personnel will have the appropriate PCL in accordance with Reference (e).

3. <u>SECURITY AGREEMENTS AND BRIEFINGS.</u>

    a. A prime contractor is responsible for issuing contracts and entering into a formal relationship with the prospective subcontractor. The prime contractor will obtain approval from the PSO before any release of SAP information. When conducting business with non-SAP briefed subcontractors, prime contractors will ensure SAP information is not inadvertently released. Any relationship with a prospective subcontractor requires prior approval by the PSO. The PSO will ensure that the association with the government activity or any SAP capability is not disclosed.

    b. Prior to the release of any SAP information, the prime contractor must brief any prospective subcontractor regarding the procurement's enhanced special security requirements. Arrangements for subcontractor SAP access will be pre-coordinated with the PSO. The CPSO will complete a subcontractor or supplier data sheet for submission to the PSO. Discussions with prospective subcontractors may occur provided the discussions are limited to general interest topics without association to the government agency and scope of effort. The CPSO will include the reason for considering a subcontractor and attaches a proposed DD Form 254 to the subcontractor or supplier data sheet. The DD Form 254 will be tailored to be consistent with the proposed support being sought and be classified based on its content.

4. <u>INDEPENDENT RESEARCH AND DEVELOPMENT (IR&D)</u>. The use of SAP information for a contractor IR&D effort occurs only with the specific written permission of the GCO. Procedures and requirements necessary for safeguarding SAP information is outlined in the DD Form 254 prepared by the PSO or designee. A letter defining the authority to conduct IR&D, a DD Form 254, and appropriate classification guidance will be provided to each contractor. Subcontracting of IR&D efforts will follow the same process as outlined in paragraph 1 of Enclosure 11 of this volume. IR&D operations and documentation that contain SAP information are subject to inspection in the same manner as other SAP classified information in the possession of the contractor.

5. <u>FOCI</u>. All SAP(s) follow established FOCI procedures outlined in Volume 3 of DoDM 5220.22 (Reference (aa)).

6. <u>NATIONAL INTEREST DETERMINATION (NID)</u>. In accordance with section 2004.22 of Title 32, Code of Federal Regulation, (Reference (ab)) a NID is required before authorizing any contractor cleared or presently in process for an FCL under a special security agreement (SSA) access to SAP information or any other proscribed information. A NID does not authorize disclosure of SAP information to a foreign government, a non-U.S. citizen, or a non-U.S. entity. Approval of NIDs are based upon an assessment of whether the release of SAP information is consistent with the national security interests of the United States. The requirement for a NID applies to new contracts, including pre-contract activities in which access to proscribed information is required, and to existing contracts when contracts are acquired by foreign interests and an SSA is the proposed foreign ownership, control, or influence mitigation method.

7. <u>DISPOSITION AND CLOSE-OUT ACTIONS.</u>

   a. CPSOs or designee will inventory, dispose of, request retention, or return for disposition all SAP material at contract completion or close-out. Request for proposals, solicitations, or bids and proposals contained in SAP files will be reviewed and screened by CPSOs in accordance with DoD Component records disposition instructions. Disposition of information by document control number will be submitted to the PSO and GCO for concurrence. Upon contract close-out, requests for retention of classified information will be submitted to the GCO through the PSO for review and approval. The contractor will not retain any SAP information unless specifically authorized in writing by the GCO. A final DD Form 254 will be issued for the storage and retention of SAP material. Storage and control requirements will be approved by the PSO.

   b. At the initiation of a closeout, termination or completion of a contract, the CPSO will consider actions for disposition of residual hardware, software, documentation, SAPF, and personnel accesses documented in a termination plan for approval by the PSO. The master classified material accountability record (log or register) will be transferred to the PSO at SAP closeout. All close out actions require final approval from the GCO and PSO.

ENCLOSURE 12

SAP TECHNOLOGY TRANSFERS

1. <u>TECHNOLOGY TRANSFERS</u>. Two primary issues must be addressed with all technology transfers. The first is to ensure that the scope of the gaining SAP SCG is sufficient to protect technology that is to be transferred. If not, the gaining SAP SCG must be updated (approved before transfer), or the transfer should not occur. The second issue is to ensure all technology to be transferred is reviewed to determine if there are any proprietary or data rights associated with the technology proposed for transfer. If so, those specific items must be clearly annotated with the appropriate data rights. The technology transfer agreement (TTA) is used to document transfers of SAP technology between U.S. government agencies. GPMs from both SAPs should maintain records of all technology transfers. TTAs can only be approved by the CA SAPCO or authorized designee. Transfers of SAP technology to a foreign government will be conducted in accordance with Foreign Disclosure Procedures in Reference (c).

2. <u>SYSTEM OR CAPABILITY TRANSFERS</u>. A system or capability transfer MOA will be prepared by the GPM, GSSO, and PSO for any system or capability transferred to or from a DoD Component from or to another DoD Component or non-DoD organization when the system or capability to be transferred requires continued resources to sustain. The system or capability transfer MOA must be approved by the CA SAPCO. The system or capability transfer MOA must include:

    a. Description of technology to be transferred (i.e., data, knowledge, equipment).

    b. Gaining and losing organizations.

    c. Roles and responsibilities.

    d. Gaining CSO.

    e. Personnel security access requirements (if beyond standard requirements).

    f. Logistics and sustainment requirements.

    g. Marking guidelines and instructions.

    h. Contracting review.

    i. Legal review.

    j. Resources necessary to sustain the SAP.

GLOSSARY

PART I. ABBREVIATIONS AND ACRONYMS

CA	Cognizant Authority
CFA	core functional area
CI	counterintelligence
CONUS	continental United States
CPM	contractor program manager
CPSO	contractor program security officer
CSO	cognizant security office
CUA	co-utilization agreement
DoDD	DoD Directive
DoDI	DoD Instruction
DoDM	DoD Manual
DSS	Defense Security Service
DTM	Directive-type memorandum
FCL	Facility Security Clearance
FOCI	foreign ownership, control, or influence
FOUO	for official use only
FWAC	fraud, waste, abuse, and corruption
GCO	government contracting officer
GPM	government program manager
GSSO	government special access program security officer
HVSACO	handle via special access channels only
IR&D	independent research and development
IS	information system
MOA	memorandum of agreement
NID	national interest determination
NISP	National Industrial Security Program
NSA/CSS	National Security Agency/Central Security Service
OA	oversight authority
OPSEC	operations security
PCL	personnel security clearance
PM	program manager
PPP	program protection plan

PSA	Principle Staff Assistant
RMF	Risk Management Framework
S	SECRET
SAP	special access program
SAPCO	special access program central office
SAPF	special access program facility
SAV	staff assistance visit
SCG	security classification guide
SCI	sensitive compartmented information
SEI	special emphasis item
SETA	security education and training awareness
SOP	standard operating procedure
SSA	special security agreement
TS	TOP SECRET
TSA	Transportation Security Administration
TSCO	TOP SECRET control officer
TTA	technology transfer agreement
USD(I)	Under Secretary of Defense for Intelligence
USG	U.S. Government
USPS	United States Postal Service

PART II. DEFINITIONS

These terms and their definitions are for the purposes of this volume.

<u>authorization.</u> The official management decision given by a senior organizational official to authorize operation of an IS and to explicitly accept the risk to organizational operations and assets, individuals, other organizations, and the United States based on the implementation of an agreed-upon set of security controls.

<u>carve-out</u>. A provision approved by the Secretary or Deputy Secretary of Defense that relieves DSS of its NISP obligation to perform industrial security oversight functions for a DoD SAP.

<u>commendable</u>. A commendable rating is assigned to a contractor or government location that have fully implemented the security requirements in an effective fashion resulting in a commendable security posture, compared with other contractor or government locations of similar size and complexity. This rating denotes a security program with strong management support, the absence of any serious security issues, and minimal administrative findings.

<u>compromise</u>. The known or suspected exposure of classified information, clandestine activities, personnel operating under cover, or sensitive installations or assets to an unauthorized person(s).

corrective action plan. A document that addresses the plan for correcting deficiencies and areas deemed unsatisfactory as noted in the self-inspection report.

CPM. The individual responsible for management of SAP(s) at the contactor location.

CPSO. The individual designated in writing by the CPM who will provide security administration and management for a SAP at a cleared defense contractor location.

cryptographic ignition key. Device or electronic key to unlock the secure mode of cryptographic equipment.

CSO. Defined in Reference (g).

deviation. Undocumented procedures or deviations of approved processes that if left uncorrected could cause increased risk of loss or compromise of classified information. This could also include: Administrative issues that could result in multiple deviations; trends; or repeat deviations may result in a finding as they pertain to compliance inspections.

finding. A deficiency that could pose a direct impact to the integrity of the SAP. Security requirements that are missing or deficient that could result in a loss or compromise of classified information.

GCO. Any person who, by appointment in accordance with applicable regulations, has the authority to enter into and administer contracts and make determinations and findings with respect thereto. The term also includes the authorized representative of the contracting officer.

GPM. Also known as a commander or a director. The GPM is responsible for management of SAP(s).

GSSO. A government, or government support position, appointed in writing at a government SAPF or organization by the Director or PM to provide security administration and management. The GSSO receives SAP guidance from the PSO.

inadvertent disclosure. The involuntary unauthorized access to classified SAP or unclassified HVSACO information by an individual without SAP access authorization.

inquiry. An inquiry consists of fact-finding and analysis conducted to determine whether or not there was a loss of classified information or whether or not unauthorized personnel had, or could have had, access to the information. The inquiry identifies the facts, characterizes the incident as an infraction or a violation, and identifies, if possible, the cause(s) and person(s) responsible, reports corrective action or a more in-depth investigation. Inquiries, generally, are initiated and conducted at the lowest level possible.

inspection official. Government official with the authority to conduct SAP compliance inspections for government and industry within their agency or organization.

investigation. Conducted for a security violation when the incident cannot be resolved via inquiry or for incidents where an in-depth and comprehensive examination of the matter is appropriate.

loss. Occurs when classified information cannot be physically located or accounted for, such as classified information or equipment is discovered missing during an audit and cannot be immediately located.

marginal. A marginal rating indicates a substandard security compliance program. This rating signifies a serious finding in one or more security areas that could contribute to the eventual compromise of classified information if left uncorrected. The contractor or government location's size, extent of classified activity, and inherent nature of the problem, are considered before assigning this rating. A compliance security review is required within a specified period to assess the actions taken to correct the findings that led to the marginal rating.

mitigation measures. Equivalent protective measures used in lieu of implementing the exact wording of this volume of this manual. Equivalent levels of protection will not be designed with the intent to reduce or lessen the security requirements of this volume.

need-to-know. A determination that a prospective recipient requires access to specific classified information in order to perform or assist in a lawful and authorized governmental function.

observation. A comment on any benchmark procedures, outstanding performers, or areas and processes that could be managed more effectively and not deficient on meeting any policy.

over flight. To fly over in an aircraft or spacecraft.

PSO. A government, or government support position appointed in writing by the appropriate Director CA SAPCO or designee, who is responsible for executing oversight and implementation of SAP security requirements for a specific SAP, group of SAPs or geographical assigned locations. The PSO is appointed to oversee and execute SAP security with responsibilities encompassing all security disciplines. The PSO exercises these responsibilities on behalf of the SAPCO.

requirements. Observations are made to identify options for the security compliance program and do not require a response or any actions to be taken.

risk management. The process that allows PSOs and security managers to balance the operational and economic costs of protective measures and achieve gains in mission capability by protecting the systems and data that support their organizations' missions.

SAP Technology Transfer. The intentional communication (sharing) of SAP knowledge, expertise, facilities, equipment, and other resources for application to military and nonmilitary systems.

SAPF. A specific physical space that has been formally accredited in writing by the responsible PSO that satisfies the criteria for generating, safeguarding, handling, discussing, and storing classified or unclassified program information, hardware, and materials.

satisfactory. The most common rating which denotes that a contractor or government location's security compliance program is in general conformity with the basic requirements. This rating may be assigned even though there were findings in one or more of the security elements. Depending on the circumstances, a satisfactory rating can be assigned even if there were isolated serious findings during the security review.

self-inspection. A physical verification of the security processes, procedures, and administrative documentation that support the SAP.

superior. Reserved for a contractor or government location that has consistently and fully implemented the security requirements in an effective fashion resulting in a superior security posture, compared with other contractor government locations of similar size and complexity. The contractor or government location must have documented procedures that heighten the security awareness of the employees and that foster a spirit of cooperation within the security community. This rating requires a sustained high level of management support for the security program and the absence of any serious security issues. For more complex contractor government locations, minimal administrative findings are allowable.

unsatisfactory. Is assigned when circumstances and conditions indicate that the contractor or government location has lost, or is in imminent danger of losing, its ability to adequately safeguard the classified material in its possession or to which it has access. This rating is appropriate when the security review indicates that the contractor or government's security compliance program can no longer preclude the disclosure of classified information to unauthorized persons. When an unsatisfactory rating is assigned, a compliance security review must be conducted after a specified interval to assess the corrective actions taken before the contractor or government location's security rating can return to the satisfactory level.

Department of Defense
MANUAL

NUMBER 5205.07, Volume 2
November 24, 2015
Incorporating Change 1, Effective February 12, 2018

USD(I)

SUBJECT: Special Access Program (SAP) Security Manual: Personnel Security

References: See Enclosure 1

1. PURPOSE

    a. Manual. This manual is composed of several volumes, each containing its own purpose. The purpose of the overall manual, in accordance with the authority in DoD Directive (DoDD) 5143.01 (Reference (a)), is to implement policy established in DoDD 5205.07 (Reference (b)), assign responsibilities, and provide security procedures for DoD SAP information.

    b. Volume. This volume:

        (1) Assigns responsibilities and provides procedures for personnel security for DoD SAPs.

        (2) Incorporates and cancels Under Secretary of Defense for Intelligence (USD(I)) Memorandum (Reference (c)).

2. APPLICABILITY. This volume applies to:

    a. OSD, the Military Departments, the Office of the Chairman of the Joint Chiefs of Staff and the Joint Staff, the Combatant Commands, the Office of the Inspector General of the Department of Defense, the Defense Agencies, the DoD Field Activities, and all other organizational entities within the DoD (referred to collectively in this volume as the "DoD Components").

    b. All DoD Component contractors and consultants that require access to DoD SAPs pursuant to the terms and conditions of their contract or agreement.

    c. Non-DoD U.S. Government departments, activities, agencies, and all other organizational entities that require access to DoD SAPs pursuant to the terms and conditions of a memorandum of agreement or other interagency agreement established with the DoD.

d. Nothing in this manual will be construed to impair the DoD Inspector General's ability to carry out its responsibilities, as delineated in DoD Directive 5106.01 (Reference (d)), pursuant to the Inspector General Act of 1978, as amended (Reference (e)).

3. <u>POLICY</u>. It is DoD policy, in accordance with Reference (b), that DoD SAPs be established and maintained when absolutely necessary to protect the most sensitive DoD capabilities, information, technologies, and operations or when required by statute.

4. <u>RESPONSIBILITIES</u>. See Enclosure 2.

5. <u>PROCEDURES</u>. See Enclosures 3 through 5.

6. <u>RELEASABILITY</u>. **Cleared for public release**. This volume is available on the ~~Internet from the DoD Issuances Website at http://www.dtic.mil/whs/directives.~~ *Directives Division Website at http://www.esd.whs.mil/DD/.*

7. <u>EFFECTIVE DATE</u>. This volume is effective November 24, 2015.

Marcel Lettre
Acting Under Secretary of Defense
for Intelligence

Enclosures
1. References
2. Responsibilities
3. Personnel Security Information
4. Special Access Program Nomination Process (SAPNP)
5. Foreign Travel Reporting
Glossary

TABLE OF CONTENTS

ENCLOSURE 1

REFERENCES

(a) DoD Directive 5143.01, "Under Secretary of Defense for Intelligence (USD(I))," October 24, 2014, as amended
(b) DoD Directive 5205.07, "Special Access Program (SAP) Policy," July 1, 2010
(c) Under Secretary of Defense for Intelligence Memorandum, "Special Access Program Nomination Process," May 20, 2013 (hereby cancelled)
(d) DoD Directive 5106.01, "Inspector General of the Department of Defense (IG DoD)," April 20, 2012, as amended
(e) Inspector General Act of 1978, as amended, Title 5, United States Code Appendix (v)
(f) DoD Instruction 3305.13, "DoD Security Education, Training, and Certification," February 13, 2014
(g) DoD Directive 5400.11, "DoD Privacy Program," October 29, 2014
(h) Executive Order 12968, "Access to Classified Information," August 2, 1995
(i) DoD Instruction 5210.91, "Polygraph and Credibility Assessment (PCA) Procedures," August 12, 2010, as amended
(j) DoD Instruction 5205.11, "Management, Administration, and Oversight of DoD Special Access Programs (SAPs)," February 6, 2013
(k) DoD 5200.2-R, "Personnel Security Program," January 1987, as amended
(k) *DoD Manual 5200.02, "Procedures for the DoD Personnel Security Program (PSP)," April 3, 2017*
(l) DoD Directive 5240.06, "Counterintelligence Awareness and Reporting (CIAR)," May 17, 2011, as amended
(m) Title 18, United States Code
(n) Title 50, United States Code
(o) DoD Instruction 5230.29, "Security and Policy Review of DoD Information for Public Release," August 13, 2014*, as amended*
(p) DoD 5220.22-M, "National Industrial Security Program Operating Manual," February 28, 2006, as amended

ENCLOSURE 2

RESPONSIBILITIES

1. <u>USD(I)</u>. The USD(I) coordinates with the Director, DoD Special Access Program Central Office (SAPCO) to assist in the development of procedures for engagement with a DoD adjudications facility to request the facility's rationale for approving any condition, deviation, or waiver associated with an individual nominated for access to a DoD SAP.

2. <u>DIRECTOR, DEFENSE SECURITY SERVICE (DSS)</u>. Under the authority, direction, and control of the USD(I) and in addition to the responsibilities in section 4 of this enclosure, the Director, DSS, conducts SAP training and education in accordance with Reference (b) and DoD Instruction 3305.13 (Reference (f)).

3. <u>~~DEPUTY~~ CHIEF MANAGEMENT OFFICER (~~D~~CMO) OF THE DEPARTMENT OF DEFENSE</u>. The ~~D~~CMO, through the Director, DoD Consolidated Adjudications Facility (CAF):

   a. Upon request, provides rationale for any condition, deviation, or waiver associated with a nominated individual's clearance in accordance with the DoD SAPCO procedures.

   b. Reviews previously unreported derogatory information in accordance with Enclosure 4 of this volume to evaluate continued clearance eligibility for individuals nominated or accessed to DoD SAP.

4. <u>DoD COMPONENT HEADS AND OSD PRINCIPAL STAFF ASSISTANTS (PSAs) WITH COGNIZANT AUTHORITY (CA) AND OVERSIGHT AUTHORITY (OA) OVER SAPs</u>. The DoD Component heads and OSD PSAs with CA and OA over SAPs implement the procedures in this volume.

5. <u>DIRECTOR, DoD SAPCO</u>. Under the authority, direction, and control of the Deputy Secretary of Defense, the Director, DoD SAPCO:

   a. Verifies that the personnel security process and training implemented by the CA and OA SAPCOs meet the standards of this volume.

   b. In coordination with the USD(I), develops procedures for engagement with the DoD adjudications facility to request the facility's rationale for approving any condition, deviation, or waiver associated with a nominated individual's clearance.

6. <u>DIRECTORS, CA SAPCO</u>. Under the authority, direction and control of their respective DoD Component heads, the Directors, CA SAPCO:

a. Exercise access approval authority (AAA) and delegate AAA, when necessary, as determined by the DoD Component head consistent with Reference (b).

b. Exercise AAA for nominated individuals who do not meet the nomination and eligibility criteria described in Enclosure 4 of this volume.

c. Designate personnel who may contact and provide information to the appropriate DoD adjudications facility.

d. Evaluate information contained in a letter of compelling need (LOCN).

e. Formally appoint individuals to serve as Special Access Program Personnel Security Officials (SPOs).

ENCLOSURE 3

PERSONNEL SECURITY INFORMATION

1. INTRODUCTION

   a. All requests for SAP access must be processed as prescribed in this volume.

   b. Nominated individuals who meet the requirements of Enclosure 4 of this volume are eligible for SAP access without further review.

   c. AAAs may disapprove the nomination based upon the individual's failure to possess the access eligibility requirements, need to know (NTK), lack of material contribution to the SAP, or based on unique risk assessment to the program. Requestors may resubmit with additional justification.

   d. Acceptable types of clearances and investigations for SAP access:

      (1) A SECRET SAP requires a minimum of a final SECRET clearance based upon either a National Agency Check with Law and Credit, or an Access National Agency Check and Inquiries or equivalent investigation, current within 5 years.

      (2) A TOP SECRET SAP requires a final TOP SECRET clearance based on a Single Scope Background Investigation (SSBI), SSBI Periodic Reinvestigation (SSBI-PR), or a Phased Periodic Reinvestigation or equivalent investigation current within 5 years.

   e. If a nominated individual with current SAP access is outside the 5-year investigative scope, the individual will retain SAP access provided that:

      (1) No potentially disqualifying information exists.

      (2) The request for periodic reinvestigation reflects as 'submitted' in the DoD system of records for security clearances within 5 years of the closed date of the last completed investigation.

   f. Potentially disqualifying information not previously reported will be assessed by the program security officer (PSO) or SPO, as appropriate.

   g. A LOCN must accompany a nomination request for individuals who do not meet criteria described in Enclosure 4 of this volume. The LOCN will describe the individual's unique skills or knowledge and the benefit the SAP will gain by accessing the individual. By listing the unique skills and knowledge, the LOCN should reflect clearly why no other individual can fulfill or is readily available to fulfill that position. The requestor will validate that a detailed justification is included in the LOCN before including it in the nomination package.

h. Nomination packages and associated personnel security databases must be administered and maintained in accordance with DoDD 5400.11 (Reference (g)). Only individuals whose duties include conducting nominated individual's reviews for access may view information contained in nomination packages.

2. SAP RECIPROCITY

a. A nominated individual with an existing DoD SAP access will not be denied access eligibility to a DoD SAP, or subsequent SAP, of the same sensitivity level provided they:

(1) Have validated NTK and can materially contribute to the new SAP.

(2) Have no new potentially disqualifying information.

(3) Meet nomination requirements for SAP access.

(4) Have all 'NO' responses on a Pre-Screening Questionnaire dated within the past 365 days.

b. A reciprocity determination for a nominated individual may only be granted when he/she has received a favorable eligibility determination from another access-granting organization. Copies of all such approvals by the CA SAPCO must be maintained with the individual's record of SAP access and be made readily available for review as necessary. This data will be captured and made a part of the individual's record in the component's system of record for SAP access.

3. PERSONNEL SECURITY ROLES

a. Requestors. Requestors will:

(1) Be accessed to the SAP for which the nominated individual is being submitted.

(2) Fill out the justification section of the Program Access Request (PAR). The justification will address why access is required by establishing NTK and the nominated individual's material contribution to the SAP.

b. SPOs. SPOs will:

(1) Be responsible for the completeness and accuracy of information submitted in nominated individual's packages.

(2) Make initial eligibility determination and, or recommendation in accordance with Enclosure 4 of this volume.

c. PSOs. PSOs will:

(1) Evaluate SPO's access eligibility recommendation, any additional information the nominated individual provides to "yes" answers on their Pre-Screening Questionnaire, and concurs or non-concurs with access to the SAP by the nominated individual. All non-concur recommendations for accesses require additional justification in the PAR remarks section or must be provided in a separate memorandum.

(2) Assess unique risks with all eligibility issues and coordinate with the respective counterintelligence (CI) support activity or the appropriate DoD adjudications facility, as necessary.

(3) Review the SAP nomination package and make an access recommendation to the AAA.

d. <u>AAAs</u>. AAAs will:

(1) Make SAP access approval or disapproval decisions, including evaluating a nominated individual's suitability when unique risk is identified in responses to the pre-screening questionnaire and coordinate with the government special access program security officer (GSSO), PSO, program manager (PM), and SAPCO as necessary.

(2) Understand that access approval is a separate and distinct action from the access eligibility determination.

(3) Be trained in their authorities, standards, and limitations in accordance with CA SAPCO guidance.

e. <u>PSOs, GSSOs, Contractor Program Security Officers (CPSOs), or SPOs</u>. PSOs, GSSOs, CPSOs, or SPOs designated by the CA SAPCO will:

(1) Forward all previously unreported derogatory information revealed in response to the pre-screening questionnaire to the DoD CAF.

(2) Advise individuals to report any information that may affect their clearance eligibility to their local security manager or special security officer for coordination with the appropriate DoD adjudications facility as outlined in this volume.

4. <u>INDOCTRINATION BRIEFINGS</u>

a. Individuals designated to conduct indoctrination briefings will ensure individuals sign the special access program indoctrination agreement (SAPIA) prior to indoctrination in accordance with Executive Order 12968 (Reference (h)) acknowledging the requirements for gaining access to SAP(s) and the SAP-specific unique requirements.

b. SAP indoctrinations will be conducted only after the PAR has been approved and the SAPIA has been signed.

c. At a minimum, the indoctrination briefings will cover the topics identified on the SAP Refresher Training Record (see http://www.dss.mil/isp/specialprograms.html) and the SAP facility standard operating procedures.

d. PSOs, GSSOs, CPSOs or their designees will give a SAP-specific security briefing to all SAP-indoctrinated personnel annually.

5. <u>POLYGRAPHS</u>. The Deputy Secretary of Defense is the approval authority for the use of polygraph examination as a mandatory access determination requirement; the requirement must be consistently applied to all candidates in accordance with DoDI 5210.91 (Reference (i)). CI-Scope polygraph examination must not be used as the only basis for granting access to DoD SAPs. Exceptions to these requirements will only be granted by the Deputy Secretary of Defense. Specific polygraph examinations to resolve issues related to SAP access eligibility will be administered in accordance with Reference (i). Per DoDI 5205.11 (Reference (j)), CI polygraph examinations are considered current when administered within the past 5 years.

6. <u>BILLET MANAGEMENT</u>. CA SAPCOs may establish or authorize SAP billet structures or access quotas that assign individual access by organization and duty position to SAPs under their cognizance. Security personnel will not count against any billet structure or access quotas.

7. <u>PERSONNEL SECURITY FILES</u>. Records must be maintained within a personnel security file for each SAP-accessed individual. The responsible PSO, GSSO, CPSO, or designee will maintain these files. The files will include, but are not limited to:

a. Pre-screening questionnaire and supplemental information as required by the CA SAPCO.

b. Consultant agreements, as necessary.

c. PARs.

d. Transfer of access (TOA) approvals.

e. SAPIAs.

f. Security education and training awareness records.

g. Foreign travel records.

h. Foreign contacts records (includes personal, business, and suspicious contact).

i. Inadvertent disclosure records.

j. Reports of security infractions and violations.

k. Potentially disqualifying information records.

l. LOCNs, as necessary.

8. <u>CONGRESSIONAL ACCESS REQUIREMENTS</u>. Guidance on congressional access to DoD SAPs is contained in Reference (b).

9. <u>INDIVIDUAL REPORTING REQUIREMENTS</u>. All SAP-accessed personnel will report to the PSO, GSSO, or CPSO any information, in addition to that identified in the pre-screening questionnaire, about themselves or others that may pose an undue risk to the SAP or possibly affect an individual's access to SAP(s). Reporting requirements are found in ~~DoD 5200.2-R~~ *DoD Manual 5200.02* (Reference (k)). Examples of reporting requirements include, but are not limited to:

a. <u>Potentially Disqualifying Information</u>. All SAP-accessed personnel will report to the PSO, GSSO, or CPSO any information that may impact ability of individuals to maintain their eligibility or properly safeguard SAP information. Examples of potentially disqualifying information include, but are not limited to:

(1) Wage garnishments.

(2) Criminal conduct (regardless of whether the individual was formally charged).

(3) Fired from a job.

(4) Any illegal drug use.

(5) Alcohol abuse.

b. <u>Foreign Travel</u>. Report all foreign travel in accordance with Enclosure 5 of this volume.

c. <u>Security Incidents</u>. Immediately report all security infractions and violations to the PSO, GSSO, or CPSO, in accordance with this volume.

d. <u>Reportable Contacts, Activities, Indicators, and Behaviors</u>. SAP- accessed personnel will report to the PSO, GGSSO, or CPSO, in accordance with Enclosure 4 of DoDD 5240.06 (Reference (l)).

10. GSSO AND CPSO REPORTING REQUIREMENTS

a. Employees Desiring Not to Perform on SAP Activities. A report will be made to the PSO upon notification by a SAP-accessed individual or an individual for whom access has been requested that they no longer wish to perform on the SAP activities.

b. Employees Refusing to Sign a SAPIA. A report will be submitted to the PSO on an individual who refuses to sign a SAPIA. If a SAPIA is not signed, SAP access will not be granted.

c. Change in Employee Status. A written report of all changes in the employment status of SAP-accessed personnel will be provided to the PSO.

11. DEPLOYED OR TEMPORARILY REASSIGNED PERSONNEL. Personnel assigned away from their home location for over 60 days will be debriefed unless they have a continued NTK at their deployment location. Exceptions to this requirement must be approved in writing by the CA SAPCO.

12. TOA. TOA is negotiated between the losing and gaining PSOs and AAAs. The TOA approval must be maintained in the personnel security file, as well as the SAPIA for the maintained accesses. Individuals with SAP access may exercise TOA under the following guidelines:

a. The individual's personnel security investigation must be current.

b. For contractors, individuals must support the same contract in order to transfer SAP access.

c. No previously unreported potentially disqualifying information exists that could affect the individual's continued eligibility for access to SAP(s).

13. DEBRIEFING ACKNOWLEDGEMENTS

a. The PSO, GSSO, or CPSO will implement a formal debriefing program when access to SAP information is no longer required.

b. Procedures for debriefing will be arranged to allow each individual the opportunity to ask questions and receive substantive answers from the individual providing the debriefing.

c. The debriefing acknowledgement portion of the SAPIA will be executed at the time of the debriefing, and forwarded to PSO or designee within 3 business days.

d. SAP-accessed personnel will be debriefed by the PSO, GSSO, CPSO, or designee, and the personnel security access database will be updated to reflect this action.

e. The debriefing will include, at a minimum, a reminder of the individual's responsibilities, as agreed to in the SAPIA, which addresses:

(1) The continuing obligations to not disclose SAP information.

(2) The SAPIA as an enforceable legal contract between the individual and the U.S. Government.

(3) All classified information, including SAP information, as the property of the U.S. Government.

(4) The penalties for espionage and unauthorized disclosure, in accordance with Titles 18 and 50, United States Code (References (m) and (n)).

(5) The obligation not to discuss, publish, or otherwise reveal information about the SAP.

(6) Acknowledgement that all future questions or concerns regarding the SAP (e.g., solicitations for information, approval to publish material based on SAP knowledge or experience) will be directed to the PSO, GSSO, or CPSO.

(a) Provide the individual with a telephone number for the PSO, GSSO, or CPSO.

(b) Where to report suspected foreign intelligence service contacts or any attempt by unauthorized individuals to solicit SAP information. Information to be provided must include last known security officer's (SO) name and contact information. The priority for reporting this information is:

<u>1</u>. PSO.

<u>2</u>. GSSO (if applicable)

<u>3</u>. CPSO (if applicable).

<u>4</u>. Respective counterintelligence element or Military Department Counterintelligence Organization (MDCO).

<u>5</u>. Nearest Federal Bureau of Investigation (FBI) office.

(8) That each provision of the agreement is severable (i.e., if one provision is declared unenforceable by a court of competent jurisdiction, all others remain in force).

(9) Though an individual has signed the debriefing acknowledgment portion of the SAPIA, they are never released from the original SAPIA unless specifically notified in writing.

(10) The requirement to return all SAP classified material and unclassified handle via special access channels only material, and the identification of all security containers to which the individual had access.

(11) How to obtain a security and policy review, pursuant to DoDI 5230.29 (Reference (o)), before publishing or other public release.

(12) What can and cannot be discussed or placed in resumes and applications for security clearances.

(13) The debriefing process, the requirement to sign the SAPIA, and the agreement that all questions about the SAPIA were addressed.

f. When access is suspended or revoked or an individual is debriefed for cause, the PSO, GSSO, or CPSO will notify all DoD Component PSOs holding interest in that individual's SAP accesses, as the GSSO or CPSO may not be aware of all SAPs to which an individual is accessed. The PSO will notify the DoD Component CA SAPCO.

g. The individual conducting the debriefing will advise individuals who refuse to sign the debriefing acknowledgment portion of the SAPIA that such refusal may affect future access to SAPs or continued clearance eligibility. Additionally, refusal to sign the debriefing acknowledgement may be cause for administrative sanctions, and it will be reported to the appropriate DoD adjudications facility and DSS, if applicable. In the event that an individual refuses to execute a debriefing acknowledgement on the SAPIA, the GSSO or CPSO must administer an oral debriefing in the presence of a witness and annotate the debriefing acknowledgment portion "ORAL DEBRIEFING CONDUCTED; INDIVIDUAL REFUSED TO SIGN." The briefer and witness sign beneath the statement attesting to this action. Immediately report this fact to the PSO. The PSO will promptly contact other organizations as required.

14. <u>ADMINSTRATIVE DEBRIEFINGS</u>. Efforts to have all SAP-accessed personnel sign a debriefing acknowledgement portion of the SAPIA may prove difficult. If attempts to locate an individual either by telephone or mail are unsuccessful, and the whereabouts of the individual cannot be determined in 30 days, the PSO, GSSO, or CPSO must administratively debrief the individual by completing the debriefing acknowledgment portion of the SAPIA with "INDIVIDUAL NOT AVAILABLE – ADMINSTRATIVELY DEBRIEFED." The appropriate database should be updated to reflect that the individual was debriefed. The PSO, GSSO or CPSO must check to ensure that no SAP information is charged out to, or in the possession of, these individuals.

15. <u>SAP ACCESS SUSPENSION AND REVOCATION</u>. The PSO in consultation with the AAA may suspend SAP accesses based on CA SAPCO guidance. The CA SAPCO will make

the decision regarding revocation of SAP access. The individual must be notified in writing of all suspension and revocation actions.

ENCLOSURE 4

SPECIAL ACCESS PROGRAM NOMINATION PROCESS (SAPNP)

1. INTRODUCTION. The SAPNP provides a timely, standardized, program-level review of the nominated individual's package for access to a DoD SAP. The SAPNP takes advantage of existing DoD resources and consists of three parts: final security clearance based on a favorable adjudication of an appropriate investigation; demonstrated NTK and material contribution and access eligibility. It is not an investigation or adjudication; rather it is a standardized security management process that applies enhanced security procedures to determine personnel suitability for access to DoD SAPs. A pre-screening questionnaire as seen in the Table must be completed to initiate the process. The nominated individual must provide additional information pertaining to each pre-screening question for which a "yes" response is provided.

Table. Pre-Screening Questionnaire

Foreign Affections	Is any of your immediate family a citizen of a country other than the United States or do you or anyone in your immediate family claim dual citizenship?
Foreign Associations	- Foreign Associations – Do you, your spouse or cohabitants have any continuing contact with citizens or dual citizens of a country other than the United States? **Reporting is not required if contact with a foreign national only occurs while in the performance of official United States Government business.** - Foreign Assets – Do you, your spouse, and/or cohabitant have any financial interest or assets in a country other than the United States?
Other Than Official Government Foreign Travel	Have you visited any foreign countries since your last completed investigation?
Personal Conduct	Has your clearance or access been suspended, denied or revoked; or have you been arrested since your last completed investigation?
Financial Responsibility	Have you had any bills referred to a collection agency, had your wages garnished, have any tax liens against you or filed for bankruptcy since your last completed investigation?

2. NOMINATION REQUIREMENTS

   a. Candidate prerequisites:

      (1) Must be a U.S. citizen.

      (2) Must possess a final TOP SECRET or SECRET clearance as appropriate to the SAP access requested.

(3) Must have a current investigation. CA SAPCO may approve exceptions to this requirement.

(4) Contractor nominated individuals must have a DD Form 254, "Department of Defense Contract Security Classification Specification," or consultant agreement authorizing SAP access in accordance with DoD 5220.22-M (Reference (p)).

b. When the requirements of paragraphs 2a(2), 2a(3), or 2a(4) of this enclosure cannot be met, requestor will submit an LOCN providing facts to support a determination that it is in the national interest for the CA or OA SAPCO to approve access.

c. Non-US citizens' access to DoD SAPs will be evaluated in accordance with Reference (b).

3. <u>NOMINATION PACKAGES</u>

a. The PAR will be used to nominate an individual for SAP access. A single PAR may be prepared for multiple SAPs under the cognizance of the same AAA.

b. Only an individual already accessed to a SAP may make a request for a nominated individual's SAP access.

c. The requestor will complete the PAR or provide the nominated individual's personal information, qualifications, his or her potential material contribution to the SAP, and NTK to the individual filling out the PAR.

d. All nomination packages for access to a DoD SAP will contain a current pre-screening questionnaire completed within the last 365 days, PAR, and supplemental information supporting 'Yes' answers.

e. The pre-screening questionnaire, and any supplemental information supplied by the nominated individual, will be maintained in the appropriate SAP access management database or personnel security file.

4. <u>NOMINATION REVIEW PROCESS</u>

a. The SAP nomination review process will be performed by an SPO, designated in writing by the CA or OA SAPCO or designee, who has completed the requisite training. The DoD SAPCO, in coordination with the DSS Center for Development of Security Excellence, will establish training guidelines and curriculum.

b. The pre-screening questionnaire will be considered current and reciprocally accepted by all DoD Components if the questionnaire was completed within the last 365 days and the answers to all questions are "No." CA SAPCO may provide guidance to the SPO pertaining to processing pre-screening questionnaire's with "Yes" responses. The CA SAPCO may require a LOCN.

c. The responsible SPO will review the nomination package for completeness and accuracy and will validate that the nominated individual meets the criteria in this volume or requires additional review for SAP access.

(1) The SPO will check the approved security clearance database to validate that the nominated individual has the appropriate clearance and the investigation completed date is current in accordance with Reference (k) and this volume.

(2) If the individual's investigation is not current or in-progress, the SPO will refer the individual to their security manager or special security officer to initiate Electronic Questionnaires for Investigations Processing (e-QIP) Standard Form (SF)-86, "Questionnaire for National Security Positions." Once reflected as submitted in the approved security clearance database, the SPO will prepare the nomination package in accordance with section 3 of this enclosure and execute the Pre-Screening Questionnaire.

(3) If the pre-screening questionnaire contains no potentially derogatory information, the SPO will make a recommendation to the AAA to approve access. If the pre-screening questionnaire contains derogatory information, the SPO will notify the PSO who will provide an access recommendation to the AAA.

(4) If the SPO determines that the answers to the pre-screening questionnaire qualify as previously unreported derogatory information, the SPO will refer the individual to their local security officer who will report the new derogatory information to the appropriate DoD adjudications facility in accordance with Reference (k).

(5) Whether or not the individual's investigation is current, if the pre-screening questionnaire contains derogatory information, then the SPO must take appropriate action in accordance with section 5 of this enclosure.

d. The SPO may not disqualify a candidate for SAP access but may recommend additional review to the PSO.

e. The government program manager (GPM) may also review the PAR for the individual's material contribution and NTK, and concur or non-concur on the PAR.

f. The AAA provides the final access decision (approval or disapproval) on the PAR.

5. <u>CONTINUED ELIGIBILITY</u>. Continued eligibility for SAP access is contingent on the individual's compliance with the following requirements:

a. Pursuant to References (k) and (p), SAP-accessed personnel have a responsibility to immediately report any changes in status that may affect their access eligibility.

b. SAP-accessed personnel annually revalidate access eligibility by either recertifying answers provided to the pre-screening questionnaire and any supplemental information provided, or by completing a new pre-screening questionnaire.

c. Failure to comply with the requirements of paragraphs 5a and 5b may result in suspension or revocation of SAP access.

d. SPOs will instruct the nominated individual to forward previously unreported derogatory information to their local security officer for submission to the appropriate DoD adjudications facility. The SPO will forward nomination package via the PSO to the appropriate CA SAPCO for decision to approve or continue access pending final disposition.

e. Any decision by the appropriate DoD adjudications facility to suspend or revoke the individual's clearance supersedes the SAPNP.

6. <u>DISAPPROVALS</u>. The AAA may disapprove nominated individuals for access by appropriately annotating and summarizing the reason for disapproval in the remarks section of the PAR. Nominated individuals disapproved for access may be resubmitted at the discretion of the requestor.

ENCLOSURE 5

FOREIGN TRAVEL REPORTING

1. <u>GENERAL</u>. SAP-accessed personnel must always be aware of their vulnerability to exploitation by foreign intelligence services. They are particularly susceptible during periods of foreign travel. Individuals must continuously exercise good judgment when contemplating travel. Failure to comply with the reporting requirements may result in suspension and possible loss of SAP access.

2. <u>OFFICIAL GOVERNMENT BUSINESS TRAVEL</u>

    a. SAP-accessed personnel will:

        (1) Report anticipated foreign travel to the GSSO or the CPSO as applicable; the traveler will ensure they report this travel to the GSSO or CPSO before leaving. Notification must be provided in sufficient time to allow for the completion of an appropriate country-specific threat awareness briefing based on the Defense Intelligence Agency (DIA) foreign intelligence threat level or CA SAPCO guidance and notification of foreign travel using the template (see http://www.dss.mil/isp/specialprograms.html).

        (2) Report any suspicious foreign contacts immediately upon return.

        (3) Within 5 business days upon return, contact the GSSO or CPSO to complete a post-travel debriefing.

    b. GSSOs or CPSOs will:

        (1) Obtain the notification of foreign travel and other relevant documentation by the SAP-accessed traveler before leaving.

        (2) Conduct pre-travel threat awareness briefings and post-travel debriefings.

        (3) Inform the PSO about any foreign travel, contacts, or security issues identified by any SAP-accessed individual.

        (4) File all completed documentation in the SAP-accessed traveler's personnel security file.

        (5) Evaluate foreign travel trends based on SAP-accessed individuals' reported travel. The travel information will be maintained in a readily accessible form.

    c. PSOs will:

(1) Upon request, provide GSSOs or CPSOs with the necessary country-specific threat information to be used during foreign travel awareness briefings.

(2) As necessary, coordinate all CSP requests, additional inquiries, and investigations.

(3) Evaluate foreign travel trends based on SAP-accessed personnel reported travel. The travel information will be maintained in a readily accessible form (i.e., a spreadsheet or database).

(4) Assess the risk of any proposed travel to a foreign country and provide defensive briefing covering potential threats specific to the location being traveled to the GSSO or CPSO, and SAP-accessed traveler as appropriate.

(5) Report suspicious travel incidents to their respective CI element or their supporting MDCO.

3. NON-OFFICIAL TRAVEL

a. SAP-accessed personnel will:

(1) Report anticipated foreign travel 30 days before the date of travel to the GSSO or CPSO to allow for the completion of appropriate country-specific threat awareness briefings based on the DIA foreign intelligence threat level or CA SAPCO guidance and notification of foreign travel using the template (see http://www.dss.mil/isp/specialprograms.html). If not practical (validated reasons are determined by the responsible GPM, GSSO, or CPSO), the SAP-accessed traveler must ensure he/she reports this travel to the GSSO or CPSO before leaving. Same day travel must be reported immediately upon return.

(2) The SAP-accessed traveler may undergo a CI polygraph examination upon return as part of the overall threat mitigation strategy.

(3) Report any suspicious foreign contacts immediately upon return.

(4) Within 5 business days upon return, contact the GSSO or CPSO to complete the notification of foreign travel debriefing.

b. CPSOs or GSSOs will:

(1) Verify justification for travel requests reported with less than 30 days notice.

(2) Review all proposed foreign travel itineraries and conduct pre-travel country-specific threat awareness briefings and post-travel debriefings.

(3) Inform the PSO about any foreign travel, contacts, or security issues identified by any SAP-accessed individual.

(4) File all foreign travel requests in the SAP-accessed traveler's personnel security file.

(5) Report any foreign travel trends to the PSO. The travel information will be maintained in a readily accessible form (i.e., a spreadsheet or database).

   c. PSO will:

(1) Verify justification for travel requests reported with less than 30 days notice.

(2) When requested, provide GSSOs or CPSOs with the necessary country-specific threat information to be used during foreign travel awareness briefings.

(3) Assess the risk of any proposed travel and develop a risk mitigation strategy.

(4) As necessary, coordinate all CSP requests, additional inquiries, and investigations.

(5) Evaluate foreign travel trends reported by the GSSO or CPSO.

(6) Report suspicious travel incidents to their respective CI element or their supporting MDCO.

4. <u>INDIVIDUALS ASSIGNED TO FOREIGN COUNTRIES</u>. SAP-accessed personnel stationed in a foreign country are not required to report travel (official or unofficial) within that country. Same day foreign travel to countries adjacent to the foreign country of station does not require prior notification, but must be reported immediately upon return. All other foreign travel will be reported in accordance with the requirements in sections 2 and 3 of Enclosure 5. Each SAP-accessed individual must inform the GSSO or CPSO of any suspicious foreign contacts encountered.

5. <u>FOREIGN TRAVEL RECORDS</u>. All foreign travel will be documented using the notification of foreign travel template and retained in the individual's personnel security file. Travel records will be retained until the individual is no longer SAP-accessed.

GLOSSARY

PART I. ABBREVIATIONS AND ACRONYMS

AAA	access approval authority
CA	cognizant authority
CAF	consolidated adjudications facility
CI	counterintelligence
CMO	*Chief Management Officer of the Department of Defense*
CPSO	contractor program security officer
CSP	counterintelligence-scope polygraph
~~DCMO~~	~~Deputy Chief Management Officer~~
DIA	Defense Intelligence Agency
DoDD	DoD Directive
DSS	Defense Security Service
e-QIP	Electronic Questionnaires for Investigations Processing
FBI	Federal Bureau of Investigation
GPM	government program manager
GSSO	government special access program security officer
LOCN	letter of compelling need
MDCO	Military Department Counter Intelligence Organization
NTK	need to know
OA	oversight authority
PAR	program access request
PM	program manager
PSA	Principal Staff Assistant

PSO	program security officer
SAP	special access program
SAPCO	special access program central office
SAPIA	special access program indoctrination agreement
SAPNP	special access program nomination process
SCI	sensitive compartmented information
SF	standard form
SO	security officer
SPO	special access program personnel security official
SSBI	single scope background investigation
SSBI-PR	single scope background investigation periodic reinvestigation
TOA	transfer of access
USD(I)	Under Secretary of Defense for Intelligence

PART II. DEFINITIONS

These terms and their definitions are for the purpose of this volume.

AAA. Individual designated by CA SAPCO to make approval and disapproval decisions for personnel nominated for access to DoD SAP.

Access National Agency Check and Inquiries. The minimum initial investigation for civilian personnel applying for non-critical sensitive national security positions.

billet. A determination that in order to meet NTK criteria, certain SAPs may elect to limit access to a predetermined number of properly cleared employees.

condition. Access eligibility granted or continued with the provision that additional security measures will be required. Such measures include, but are not limited to, additional security monitoring, access restrictions, submission of periodic financial statements, and attendance at counseling sessions.

CSP. A screening polygraph examination that uses relevant questions limited to prescribed CI issues.

current investigation. An investigation not older than 5 years from the closed date of the previous investigation. Individuals who have submitted their SF 86 via e-QIP and the approved security clearance database shows submitted or open investigation prior to the expiration of the previous investigation are deemed to be current.

deviation. Access eligibility granted or continued despite either a significant gap in coverage or scope in the investigation or out-of-date investigation. "Significant gap" for this purpose means either complete lack of coverage for a period of 6 months or more within the recent 5 years investigated or the lack of an FBI name check or technical check, or the lack of one or more relevant checks.

e-QIP. A web-based automated system that was designed to facilitate the processing of standard investigative forms used when conducting background investigations for federal security, suitability, fitness and credentialing purposes. e-QIP allows the user to electronically enter, update, and transmit their personal investigative data over a secure internet connection to a requesting agency.

equivalent investigation. An investigation equal to or greater in scope.

expanded-scope screening. A screening polygraph examination that includes the questions from a CSP polygraph and questions related to falsification of security forms, involvement with illegal drugs, and criminal activity.

immediate family. A spouse, parent, sibling, child, or cohabitant. This includes any step-parents, half and step-siblings, and step-children of the subject.

issue-based examination. An issue-based polygraph examination that is predicated on an allegation or a specific issue under investigation.

LOCN. A written description of an individual's unique skills or knowledge, the benefit the SAP will gain by accessing the individual, and why no other individual can fulfill or is readily available to fulfill that position.

National Agency Check With Law and Credit Check. The minimum initial investigation for military accessions and contractor personnel that require eligibility for a Confidential or Secret security clearance.

periodic reinvestigation. A reinvestigation conducted at pre-determined intervals for personnel occupying non-critical sensitive or critical sensitive national security positions.

personnel security. The security discipline that assesses the loyalty, reliability, and trustworthiness of individuals for initial and continued eligibility for access to classified information or assignment in sensitive positions.

requestor. An individual who requests SAP access for an individual not higher than the classification level and SAPs that the requestor is assessed to, and completes the justification section of the PAR.

<u>revocation.</u> Rescinding SAP access when a currently SAP-accessed individual is determined to be ineligible.

<u>SPO.</u> Individual that has been trained and nominated to apply enhanced security procedures to determine personnel eligibility for access to DoD SAPs in accordance with this volume.

<u>SSBI.</u> The minimum investigation for personnel applying for special or critical-sensitive national security positions or for personnel that require eligibility for a Top Secret security clearance.

<u>SSBI-PR.</u> A modification to the investigative standards for SSBI – periodic reinvestigations. Applies to all civilian and military personnel, as well as consultants, contractors, licensees, certificate holders, grantees, and their employees, and all other individuals who require access to SCI and SAPs.

<u>suspension of access.</u> An action taken regarding a currently SAP-accessed individual, as a result of certain personnel security conditions or questionable circumstances.

<u>system of record.</u> Defined in Reference (g).

<u>TOA.</u> An action that enables an individual to retain SAP accesses when the individual is transferred from one location to another for continued SAP access.

Department of Defense
MANUAL

NUMBER 5205.07, Volume 3
April 23, 2015
Incorporating Change 2, Effective February 12, 2018

USD(I)

SUBJECT: DoD Special Access Program (SAP) Security Manual: Physical Security

References: See Enclosure 1

1. PURPOSE

a. <u>Manual</u>. This manual is composed of several volumes, each containing its own purpose. The purpose of the overall manual, in accordance with the authority in DoD Directive (DoDD) 5143.01 (Reference (a)), is to implement policy established in DoDD 5205.07 (Reference (b)), assign responsibilities, and provide security procedures for DoD SAP information.

b. <u>Volume</u>. This volume:

(1) Implements policy established in DoD Instruction (DoDI) 5205.11 (Reference (c).

(2) Assigns responsibilities and provides procedures for physical security for DoD SAPs.

2. APPLICABILITY

a. This volume applies to:

(1) OSD, the Military Departments, the Office of the Chairman of the Joint Chiefs of Staff and the Joint Staff, the Combatant Commands, the Office of the Inspector General of the Department of Defense, the Defense Agencies, the DoD Field Activities, and all other organizational entities within the DoD (referred to collectively in this volume as the "DoD Components").

(2) All DoD Component contractors and consultants that require access to DoD SAPs pursuant to the terms and conditions of the contract or agreement.

(3) Non-DoD U.S. Government departments, activities, agencies, and all other organizational entities that require access to DoD SAPs pursuant to the terms and conditions of a memorandum of agreement or other interagency agreement established with the DoD.

b. Nothing in this volume will be construed to contradict or inhibit compliance with chapter 126 of Title 42, United States Code (Reference (d)) or building codes.

3. <u>POLICY</u>. It is DoD policy in accordance with Reference (b) that DoD SAPs be established and maintained when absolutely necessary to protect the most sensitive DoD capabilities, information, technologies, and operations or when required by statute.

4. <u>RESPONSIBILITIES</u>. See Enclosure 2.

5. <u>PROCEDURES</u>

a. All applicable DoD Components and entities specified in paragraph 2a will follow Reference (b), the general procedures in this volume, and the standards and processing procedures and templates on the Defense Security Service (DSS) Website (http://www.dss.mil/isp/specialprograms.html). See Enclosure 3 concerning the physical standards for protecting SAP information.

b. SAP-accredited areas that are presently accredited, under construction, or in the approval process at the effective date of this volume will not require modification to conform to these standards. SAP-accredited areas undergoing major modification may be required to comply entirely with the provisions of this volume. Approval for such modifications will be requested and approved in accordance with Enclosure 3 of this volume.

6. <u>RELEASABILITY</u>. **Cleared for public release**. This volume is available on the ~~DoD Issuances Website at http://www.dtic.mil/whs/directives.~~ *Directives Division website at http://www.esd.whs.mil/DD/.*

7. <u>EFFECTIVE DATE</u>. This volume is effective April 23, 2015.

Michael G. Vickers
Under Secretary of Defense for Intelligence

Enclosures
    1. References
    2. Responsibilities
    3. General Procedures
Glossary

TABLE OF CONTENTS

ENCLOSURE 1

REFERENCES

(a) DoD Directive 5143.01, "Under Secretary of Defense for Intelligence (USD(I))," October 24, 2014, as amended
(b) DoD Directive 5205.07, "Special Access Program (SAP) Policy," July 1, 2010
(c) DoD Instruction 5205.11, "Management, Administration, and Oversight of DoD Special Access Programs (SAPs)," February 6, 2013
(d) Chapter 126 of Title 42, United States Code
(e) Office of the National Counterintelligence Executive, "Technical Specifications for Construction and Management of Sensitive Compartmented Information Facilities, Version 1.2," April 23, 2012
(f) Intelligence Community Directive 705, "Sensitive Compartmented Information Facilities," May 26, 2010
(g) DoD Instruction 5240.05, "Technical Surveillance Countermeasures (TSCM)," April 3, 2014
(h) DoD Manual 5105.21, Volume 2, "Sensitive Compartmented Information (SCI) Administrative Security Manual: Administration of Physical Security, Visitor Control, and Technical Security," October 19, 2012
(i) Federal Specification FF-L 2740B, "Locks, Combination, Electromechanical," June 15, 2011[1]
(j) Committee on National Security Systems Instruction 7000, "TEMPEST Countermeasures for Facilities," May 2004[2]
(k) DoD Manual 5200.01, Volume 3, "DoD Information Security Program: Protection of Classified Information," February 24, 2012, as amended
(l) Committee on National Security Systems Advisory Memorandum TEMPEST/01-13, "Red/Black Installation Guidance," January 17, 2014[3]

---

[1] View at NIPRNET http://www.gsa.gov/portal/content/103856#FederalSpecifications
[2] View at SIPRNET at http://www.iad.nsa.smil.mil/resources/library/cnss_section/cnss_instructions.cfm
[3] View at SIPRNET at http://www.iad.nsa.smil.mil/resources/library/cnss_section/pdf/TEMPEST_CNASSAM_01_13.pdf

ENCLOSURE 2

RESPONSIBILITIES

1. <u>UNDER SECRETARY OF DEFENSE FOR INTELLIGENCE (USD(I))</u>. The USD(I) develops and maintains this volume.

2. <u>DIRECTOR, DSS</u>. Under the authority, direction, and control of the USD(I), the Director, DSS, conducts security oversight functions to validate the certification and accreditation of industrial special access program facilities (SAPFs) in accordance with Reference (c).

3. <u>DIRECTOR, DoD SPECIAL ACCESS PROGRAM CENTRAL OFFICE (SAPCO)</u>. Under the authority, direction, and control of the Deputy Secretary of Defense, the Director, DoD SAPCO, verifies that the physical security measures implemented by the congressional committees processing and storing DoD SAP information meet the standards of this volume.

4. <u>DoD COMPONENT HEADS AND OSD PRINCIPAL STAFF ASSISTANTS (PSAs) WITH COGNIZANT AUTHORITY (CA) AND OVERSIGHT AUTHORITY (OA) OVER SAPs</u>. The DoD Component heads and OSD PSAs with CA and OA over SAPs implement the procedures in this volume.

5. <u>DIRECTORS OF THE DoD COMPONENT SAPCOs AND DIRECTORS OF THE PSA SAPCOs WITH CA AND OA OVER SAPs</u>. Directors of the DoD Component SAPCOs and Directors of the PSA SAPCOs with CA and OA over SAPs:

   a. Establish training standards for and designate properly trained special access program facility accrediting officials (SAOs).

   b. Grant waivers to the standards stipulated in this volume based on a risk assessment and operational requirements.

ENCLOSURE 3

GENERAL PROCEDURES

1. GENERAL

    a. The procedures in this enclosure are minimum standards for providing physical security in the DoD Components. It is at the discretion of the DoD Components to provide more specific guidance.

    b. A SAPF, temporary special access program facility (T-SAPF), special access program compartmented area (SAPCA), special access program working area (SAPWA), or special access program temporary secure working area (SAPTSWA) will be accredited by a CA SAPCO designated SAO before receiving, generating, processing, using, or storing SAP classified information, as appropriate to the accreditation.

        (1) The government SAP security officer (GSSO) or the program security officer (PSO) and contractor program security officer (CPSO) responsible for the daily operation of the facility will notify the SAO of any activity that affects the accreditation. PSOs may perform SAO functions when designated by the CA SAPCO.

        (2) The physical security safeguards established in the Office of the National Counterintelligence Executive Technical Specifications (Reference (e)) and Intelligence Community Directive 705 (Reference (f)) are the physical standards for protection of SAP information. Construction of SAPFs, T-SAPFs, SAPCAs, SAPWAs, and SAPTSWAs will conform to the equivalent sensitive compartmented information facility (SCIF), T-SCIF, CA, SWA, TSWA, as defined in Reference (e), unless variations are specifically noted in this volume.

    c. Security standards will apply to all proposed SAP areas and will be coordinated with the SAO for guidance and approval. Location of construction or fabrication does not exclude a SAPF, T-SAPF, SAPCA, SAPWA or SAPTSWA from security standards and or review and approval by the SAO.

    d. The Director, CA SAPCO must approve waivers for imposing safeguards exceeding a standard, even when the additional safeguards are based on risk.

    e. When a SAPF, T-SAPF, SAPCA, SAPWA, and SAPTSWA are operational, only appropriately accessed SAP indoctrinated individual(s) will occupy them.

    f. TEMPEST security measures must be considered if electronic processing will occur in the SAPF, T-SAPF, SAPCA, SAPWA, and SAPTSWA. The SAO will submit plans to a certified TEMPEST technical authority (CTTA) for assessment.

g. DoD contractors under the National Industrial Security Program will possess a facility security clearance (FCL) validated by the PSO and have an accredited SAPF, T-SAPF, SAPCA, SAPWA, and SAPTSWA before receiving, generating, processing, using, or storing SAP classified information. The classification level of the SAP information within the SAPF, T-SAPF, SAPCA, SAPWA, and SAPTSWA cannot exceed the classification level of the FCL. The CPSO will notify the PSO of any activity that affects the FCL or SAP accreditation.

2. <u>SAP ACCREDITED AREAS</u>. Areas where SAP material is processed, stored, discussed, manufactured, or tested may fall into one of these categories: SAPF, T-SAPF, SAPCA, SAPWA, and SAPTSWA.

a. A SAPF (to include a T-SAPF) or SAPCA is an accredited area where SAP materials may be stored, used, discussed, manufactured, or electronically processed. SAPFs or SAPCAs may include fixed facilities, mobile platforms, and modular or prefabricated structures. Physical security protection for a SAPF or SAPCA will prevent as well as detect unauthorized visual, acoustical, technical, and physical access by unauthorized persons. Physical security criteria are governed by whether or not the SAPF or SAPCA is located in the United States and according to the operational criteria of closed storage, open storage, or continuous operations. Reference (e) details the specific construction, physical controls, and alarm systems for each situation.

b. A SAPCA is required when different compartmented programs are sharing the same SAPF and SCIF and not all personnel are cross-briefed. CA SAPCO designated SAO concurrence with visual, acoustic, and access control measures is required. Compartmented area personnel do not have to be briefed to the accreditation level of the parent SAPF or SCIF. However, appropriate operating procedures must be approved by the responsible PSO(s) or GSSOs that ensure separation of non-cleared personnel from the various SAPs operating in the SAPF or SCIF and the SAPCA. DoD SAPs will only be stored, used, discussed, manufactured, or electronically processed in Compartmented Area levels 2 or 3, as defined in Reference (f).

c. A SAPWA is an accredited area used for discussing, handling, or processing SAP. Storage of SAP material in a SAPWA is not authorized.

d. A SAPTSWA is an accredited area where handling, discussing, or processing of SAP is limited to less than 40 hours per month and the accreditation is limited to 12 months or less. Re-accreditation as a SAPTSWA requires a new physical inspection of the area. Storage of SAP material in a SAPTSWA is not authorized.

3. <u>RISK MANAGEMENT</u>

a. If, during a preconstruction and inspection phase, it is the determined that full compliance with the minimum standards contained in this volume is not possible, the SAO will select appropriate mitigating actions or activities based on analytical risk management process defined in Reference (e).

b. A determination made by the SAO that a facility's security SAP consists of layered and complementary security controls sufficient to deter and detect unauthorized entry and movement within the facility. Security in depth (SID) describes the factors that enhance the probability of detection before actual penetration to the SAPF. The existence of a layer or layers of security that offer mitigations for risks may be accepted by the SAO. An important factor in determining risk is whether layers of security already exist at the areas where SAP material is processed, stored, discussed, manufactured, or tested.

4. PHYSICAL SECURITY PRECONSTRUCTION REVIEW AND APPROVAL. SAOs will review physical security preconstruction plans for SAPF, T-SAPF, SAPCA, SAPWA, and SAPTSWA construction, expansion, or modification to ensure compliance with applicable construction criteria standards in chapters 3 through 11 of Reference (e). Any proposed mitigation and SID will be documented in the plans. The approval or disapproval of a physical security preconstruction plan will be in writing and retained in the requester's files.

a. The requester will submit the appropriate checklist from Reference (e) for all SAP accreditations to the respective SAO for review and approval. The completed checklist will be classified in accordance with specific SAP security classification guidance.

b. The SAP fixed facility checklist (FFC) submission will include floor plans, diagrams of electrical and communications wiring; heating, ventilation, and air conditioning connections; security equipment layout (to include the location of intrusion detection equipment) and SID. All diagrams or drawings must be submitted on legible and reproducible media.

c. The SAPCA checklist should be accompanied by the FFC, associated floor plans, and current accreditation of the parent SAPF or SCIF with particular emphasis on the placement of intrusion detection system sensors, if required, and type of locks and access control used or proposed for the SAPCA.

5. SAP CONSTRUCTION PROCEDURES

a. The SAO will:

(1) Review and approve or disapprove the design concept, construction security plan (CSP), and final design for each construction project before the start of construction in accordance with Reference (e) and this volume.

(2) Physically inspect a SAPF, T-SAPF, SAPCA, SAPWA, and SAPTSWA before accreditation in accordance with construction standards in Reference (e) and this volume.

(3) Provide construction advice and guidance as required.

(4) Inspect SAPFs, T-SAPFs, SAPCAs, SAPWAs, and SAPTSWAs at an interval as determined by the CA SAPCO and withdraw accreditation when situations dictate.

(5) Approve and document mitigations commensurate with the standards in Reference (e).

(6) Recommend waivers of physical security safeguards to the Director, CA SAPCO.

(7) Ensure mitigating strategies are implemented and documented in the CSP in Reference (e) when using non-U.S. citizen workers.

(8) Request construction surveillance technicians to supplement site access controls, implement screening and inspection procedures, and monitor construction and personnel in accordance with Reference (e).

b. The site security manager will:

(1) Advise the SAO of the potential for variation from the requirements of this volume.

(2) In consultation with the SAO, develop a CSP regarding implementation of the standards of this volume and Reference (e). The CSP will include a plan of action and milestones required to document the SAPF, T-SAPF, SAPCA, SAPWA, and SAPTSWA construction from start to finish.

(3) Conduct periodic security inspections for the duration of the SAPF, T-SAPF, SAPCA, SAPWA, and SAPTSWA construction to ensure compliance with the CSP.

(4) Prepare necessary waiver requests and forward to the SAO for further processing.

(5) Investigate and document security violations or deviations from the CSP. Notify the PSO of security violations and the SAO of deviations from the CSP within 24 hours of incident detection

. (6) Implement physical access control measures in accordance with Reference (e).

c. CTTAs will:

(1) Review construction or renovation plans to determine if TEMPEST countermeasures are required and recommend solutions. To the maximum extent practicable, TEMPEST mitigation requirements will be incorporated into the design.

(2) Provide the SAO with documented results of the review with recommendations.

d. Construction security requirements are detailed in Reference (e) and Enclosure 3 of this volume.

6. ACCREDITATION

a. The procedures for establishment and accreditation of a SAPF, T-SAPF, SAPCA, SAPWA, and SAPTSWA will follow guidelines distributed by the CA SAPCO.

b. The SAO will inspect any SAP area before accreditation. Periodic re-inspections will be conducted based on threat, physical modifications, sensitivity of SAPs, and past security performance, but will be conducted no less frequently than every 3 years. Inspections, announced or unannounced, may occur at any time. The current FFC will be reviewed during inspections to ensure continued compliance. Technical surveillance countermeasures (TSCM) evaluations may be required at the discretion of the SAO, as conditions warrant, and will be implemented in accordance with DoDI 5240.05 (Reference (g)). Inspection reports will be retained within the SAPF, T-SAPF, SAPCA, SAPWA, and SAPTSWA and by the SAO. All SAPFs, T-SAPFs, SAPCAs, SAPWAs, and SAPTSWAs will maintain, on site, current copies of:

(1) SAP FFC and supporting documentation.

(2) Any accreditation documents (e.g., physical, TEMPEST, and information systems) and copies of any waivers granted by the CA SAPCO.

(3) SAPF accreditation approval documentation (including mitigations and waivers).

(4) TSCM reports, for the entire period of SAPF, T-SAPF, SAPCA, SAPWA, and SAPTSWA accreditation.

(5) Operating procedures and any security documentation (including information system security authorization package, co-utilization agreements (CUAs), appointment letters, memorandums of agreement, and emergency action plans).

7. CO-UTILIZATION

a. DoD Components that want to co-utilize a SAPF, T-SAPF, SAPCA, SAPWA, and SAPTSWA will accept the current accreditation of the responsible agency if accredited without waiver to the standards in this volume. Prospective tenant activities will be informed of all mitigations and waivers to the requirements of this volume before co-utilization. Any security enhancements required by an agency or department requesting co-utilization should be funded by that organization, and must be approved by the CA SAPCO before implementation. A CUA must be established before occupancy.

b. Before creating a SAPCA in a SCIF or using sensitive compartmented information (SCI) in a SAPF or SAPCA, a CUA will be established in accordance with Enclosure 2 of Volume 2 of DoD Manual (DoDM) 5105.21 (Reference (h)).

8. PHYSICAL ACCESS CONTROLS

   a. Each SAPF, T-SAPF, SAPCA, SAPWA, and SAPTSWA will have procedures for identification and control of visitors seeking physical access in accordance with this volume and Reference (e). Personal introduction and identification should be used to the maximum extent.

   b. When all individuals within a SAPF, T-SAPF, SAPCA, SAPWA, and SAPTSWA cannot be personally identified, a badging system may be required by the PSO. This normally occurs when a SAPF, T-SAPF, SAPCA, SAPWA, and SAPTSWA hosts more than 25 people.

      (1) When a badge system is considered necessary, it will be documented in the standard operating procedures (SOPs) and address topics such as badge accountability, storage, disposition, destruction, format, and use.

      (2) If card readers are used in conjunction with badges and a means exists to lock out lost, unused, and relinquished badges, the PSO or GSSO may negate the requirements in this section for badge inventory, accountability, and destruction.

   c. When not occupied, SAPFs and T-SAPFs will be alarmed in secure mode and secured with an approved General Services Administration (GSA) FF-L2740A combination lock in accordance with Federal Specification FF-L 2740B (Reference (i)).

   d. Access control to a SAPCA will be accomplished by mechanical or electronic access control devices only. Spin-dial combination locks (e.g., XO series locks) will not be installed on SAPCA doors and independent alarm systems will not be installed in a SAPCA. Intrusion sensors will be installed when the SAPCA includes an exterior boundary wall of the parent SAPF or SCIF.

9. CONTROL OF COMBINATIONS

   a. Combinations to locks will not be the same throughout a SAPF, T-SAPF, SAPCA, SAPWA, and SAPTSWA (e.g., doors, vaults).

   b. Combinations to locks installed on security containers, safes, perimeter doors, windows, and any other opening will be changed when:

      (1) A combination lock is first installed or used.

      (2) A combination has been subjected, or believed to have been subjected, to compromise.

      (3) A person knowing the combination no longer requires access to it unless other sufficient controls exist to prevent access to the lock.

      (4) The PSO, GSSO, or CPSO considers the change necessary.

c. When the lock is taken out of service, the combination will be reset to 50-25-50. Unserviceable high-security padlocks, keys, and cylinders will be controlled until properly destroyed. These high-security padlocks, cylinders, and keys can be sent to the DoD Lock Program for disposal at the following addresses:

(1) For Navy, Marine Corps, and Coast Guard, ship via registered mail to:

Commanding Officer
Naval Surface Warfare Center,
Crane, IN 47522-5010
(Code GXQS)

(2) For all other DoD Components, ship via registered mail to:

DoD Lock Program (HSPS)
1100 23rd Avenue
Port Hueneme, CA 93043-4370

d. All combinations to the SAPF, T-SAPF, SAPCA, SAPWA, and SAPTSWA entrance doors should be stored in a different SAPF, T-SAPF, SAPCA, SAPWA, and SAPTSWA accredited at the same or higher classification level and handling caveat. When this is not feasible, the PSO or GSSO will prescribe alternative storage locations.

e. Safe combinations will be safeguarded at the highest level of classification and handling caveats of the material stored.

10. ENTRY-EXIT INSPECTIONS. The SAPF, T-SAPF, SAPCA, SAPWA, and SAPTSWA will have procedures for inspecting personal belongings and vehicles at the entry and exit points, or at other designated areas, and points of entry to the building or site. Inspections will deter the unauthorized removal of classified material and the introduction of prohibited items or contraband. Legal counsel should review all personnel inspection procedures before distribution.

11. CONTROL OF ELECTRONIC DEVICES AND OTHER ITEMS

a. The SOP will contain guidance for control of portable electronic devices (PEDs) and other items introduced into or removed from the SAPF, T-SAPF, SAPCA, SAPWA, and SAPTSWA.

b. The following PEDs without loadable data storage capabilities are authorized within the SAPF, T-SAPF, SAPCA, SAPWA, and SAPTSWA. Medical devices with a two-way capability require approval by the PSO or SAO.

(1) Electronic calculators, spell checkers, language translators, etc.

(2) Receive-only pagers.

(3) Audio and video playback devices.

(4) Receive-only radios.

(5) Devices that do not transfer, receive, store, or generate data (text, audio, video, etc.).

c. Designated areas may be identified at the entry point to all SAP areas for the storage of PEDs. Where PED storage areas or containers are allowed by the PSO to be within the SAPF, T-SAPF, SAPCA, SAPWA, and SAPTSWA, the PEDs will be turned off. These designated PED storage areas or containers will be confined to designated "non-discussion" areas.

d. Mission-essential government- or contractor- owned PEDs introduced into the SAPF, T-SAPF, SAPCA, SAPWA, and SAPTSWA will be approved by the PSO and AO or designee in accordance with Reference (e) before entering the SAPF, T-SAPF, SAPCA, SAPWA, and SAPTSWA.

e. The prohibition of PEDs in SAPFs, T-SAPFs, SAPCAs, SAPWAs, and SAPTSWAs does not apply to those needed by persons with disabilities or for medical or health reasons (e.g., motorized wheelchairs, hearing aids, heart pacemakers, amplified telephone headsets, teletypewriters for the hearing impaired). The PSO, GSSO, or CPSO will establish procedures within the SOP for notification that such equipment is being brought into the SAPF, T-SAPF, SAPCA, SAPWA, and SAPTSWA.

f. Emergency personnel or first responders and their equipment, including devices carried by emergency medical personnel, responding to a medical crisis within a SAPF, T-SAPF, SAPCA, SAPWA, and SAPTSWA, will be admitted without regard to their security clearance status. Emergency personnel will be escorted to the degree practical. As appropriate, arrangements will be made for the debriefing of emergency personnel as soon as possible.

g. Waivers to this policy must be in writing and approved by the Director, CA SAPCO or designee. Requests for waivers must be submitted by the SAO and:

(1) Approved on a case-by-case basis based on mission requirements.

(2) Coordinated with the appropriate authorizing official for each affected information system within the SAP accredited area.

(3) Identify mitigations.

(4) Identify risks (after mitigation) to classified information.

h. If the CA SAPCO approves the waiver, the facility SOP will be revised to define the procedures and guidance for control of PEDs and other items introduced into or removed from the SAPF, T-SAPF, SAPCA, SAPWA, and SAPTSWA. In addition, any tenant SAP PSOs will be notified in writing and informed the facility is accredited with waiver for appropriate action by the tenant CA SAPCO.

12. <u>TEMPEST REQUIREMENTS</u>

a. When compliance with TEMPEST standards is required, the PSO or SAO will issue specific guidance in accordance with current national directives that afford consideration to realistic, validated local threats as well as cost effectiveness.

b. A CTTA must conduct or validate all TEMPEST countermeasure reviews in accordance with Reference (e) and the Committee on National Security Instruction 7000 (Reference (j)).

c. If a TEMPEST countermeasure review has been completed, and the CTTA has determined that TEMPEST countermeasures are required, the CTTA will recommend the most cost-effective countermeasure that will contain compromising emanations within the inspectable space.

d. Only those TEMPEST countermeasures recommended by CTTA and authorized by the government program manager or government contracting official should be implemented. The processing of classified national security information as defined in in Volume 3 of DoDM 5200.01 (Reference (k)) or the submission of information for a TEMPEST countermeasure review does not imply a requirement to implement TEMPEST countermeasures. TEMPEST countermeasures that CTTA may be recommend include, but are not limited to:

(1) The use of shielded enclosures or architectural shielding.

(2) The use of equipment that has TEMPEST profiles or TEMPEST zones that match the inspectable space, distance, or zone respectively.

(3) The use of RED and BLACK separation installation guidance in accordance with Committee on National Security Systems Advisory Memorandum TEMPEST/01-13 (Reference (l)).

e. Telephone line filters, power filters, and non-conductive disconnects are not required for TEMPEST purposes, unless recommended by a CTTA as part of a TEMPEST countermeasure requirement. Telephone line disconnects, not to be confused with telephone line filters, may be required for non-TEMPEST purposes.

13. <u>TWO PERSON INTEGRITY (TPI)</u>. TPI mandates the minimum of two indoctrinated persons at all times in a SAPF, T-SAPF, SAPCA, SAPWA, and SAPTSWA. This security protection can only be authorized by the Director, CA SAPCO or designee, and reflected in the SOP.

GLOSSARY

PART I. ABBREVIATIONS AND ACRONYMS

CA	cognizant authority
CSP	construction security plan
CPSO	contractor program security officer
CTTA	certified TEMPEST technical authority
CUA	co-utilization agreement
DoDD	DoD Directive
DoDI	DoD Instruction
DoDM	DoD Manual
DSS	Defense Security Service
FCL	facility security clearance
FFC	fixed facility checklist
GSA	General Services Administration
GSSO	government SAP security officer
OA	oversight authority
PED	portable electronic device
PSA	principal staff assistant
PSO	program security officer
SAO	special access program facility accrediting official
SAP	special access program
SAPCA	special access program compartmented area
SAPCO	Special Access Program Central Office
SAPF	special access program facility
SAPTSWA	special access program temporary secure working area
SAPWA	special access program working area
SCI	sensitive compartmented information
SCIF	sensitive compartmented information facility
SID	security in depth
SOP	standard operating procedures
TPI	two person integrity
T-SAPF	temporary special access program facility
TSCM	technical surveillance countermeasures
USD(I)	Under Secretary of Defense for Intelligence

PART II. DEFINITIONS

Unless otherwise indicated, these terms and their definitions are for the purposes of this volume.

accreditation. The formal approval of a specific place, referred to as a SAPF, that meets prescribed physical, technical, and personnel security standards.

closed storage. The storage of SAP material in properly secured GSA-approved security containers within an accredited SAPF.

continuous operation. This condition exists when a SAPF is staffed 24 hours every day.

co-utilization. Two or more organizations that share the same SAPF.

CTTA. Defined in Reference (j).

open storage. The storage of SAP material within a SAPF in any configuration other than within GSA-approved security containers.

RED and BLACK separation. The segregation of equipment that processes classified information (RED) from equipment that processes unclassified information (BLACK) in unique, isolated areas. This partition prevents the inadvertent transmission of classified data over telephone lines, power lines, signal lines, and electrical components, circuits, and communication media.

SAO. A properly trained SAP facility accrediting official designated by the CA SAPCO to physically inspect and review and approve or disapprove physical security preconstruction plans for a SAPF, T-SAPF, SAPCA, and SAPWA or SAPTSWA before accreditation.

SAPCA. A room or set of rooms located within a SAPF or SCIF that is designed to enforce need-to-know. A SAPCA is required when different compartmented programs are sharing the same SAPF or SCIF and when not all personnel are cross-briefed.

SAPF. An accredited area, room, group of rooms, building, or installation where SAP materials may be stored, used, discussed, manufactured, or electronically processed. SAPFs include, but are not limited to, fixed facilities, mobile platforms, prefabricated structures, containers, modular applications, or other new or emerging applications and technologies that may meet performance standards for use in SAPF construction.

SAPTSWA. An accredited area normally used for meetings involving the discussion or processing of SAP information, when use is limited to less than 40 hours per month.

SAPWA. An accredited area used for discussing, handling, or processing SAP, but where storage is not authorized.

<u>SCI</u>. Classified information concerning or derived from intelligence sources, methods, or analytical processes, which is required to be handled exclusively within formal control systems established by the Director of National Intelligence.

<u>SCIF</u>. An accredited area, room, group of rooms, building, or installation where SCI may be stored, used, discussed, or electronically processed.

<u>SID</u>. A determination made by the SAO that a facility's security SAP consists of layered and complementary security controls sufficient to deter and detect unauthorized entry and movement within the facility. SID describes the factors that enhance the probability of detection before actual penetration to the SAPF. The existence of a layer or layers of security that offer mitigations for risks may be accepted by the SAO.

<u>site security manager</u>. Defined in Reference (f).

<u>TEMPEST</u>. The investigation and study of compromising emanations.

<u>T-SAPF</u>. SAPF designed to be temporary or such as those at sites for contingency operations, emergency operations, and tactical military operations meeting the requirements of chapter 6 of Reference (e).

<u>TSCM</u>. Techniques and measures to detect, neutralize, and exploit a wide variety of hostile and foreign penetration technologies that are used to obtain unauthorized access to classified and sensitive information.

<u>TSCM evaluations</u>. A physical, electronic, and visual examination to detect technical surveillance devices, technical security hazards, and attempts at clandestine penetration.

<u>vault</u>. A room(s) used for the storing, handling, discussing, or processing of SAP information and constructed to afford maximum protection against unauthorized entry.

<u>waiver</u>. An exemption to the security requirements of this volume.

Department of Defense

MANUAL

NUMBER 5205.07, Volume 4
October 10, 2013
Incorporating Change 1, Effective May 9, 2018

USD(I)

SUBJECT: Special Access Program (SAP) Security Manual: Marking

References: See Enclosure 1

1. <u>PURPOSE</u>

a. <u>Manual</u>. This Manual is composed of several volumes, each containing its own purpose. The purpose of the overall Manual, in accordance with the authority in DoD Directive (DoDD) 5143.01 (Reference (a)), is to implement policy established in DoDD 5205.07 (Reference (b)), assign responsibilities, and provide security procedures for DoD SAP information.

b. <u>Volume</u>. This Volume:

(1)
(Reference (e)).

(2) Cancels Directive-Type Memorandum 07-021 (Reference (f)).

2. APPLICABILITY. This Volume applies to:

a. OSD, the Military Departments, the Office of the Chairman of the Joint Chiefs of Staff and the Joint Staff, the Combatant Commands, the Office of the Inspector General of the Department of Defense, the Defense Agencies, the DoD Field Activities, and all other organizational entities (hereinafter referred to collectively as the "DoD Components").

b. All DoD Component contractors and consultants that require access to DoD SAPs, pursuant to the terms and conditions of the contract or agreement.

c. Non-DoD U.S. Government departments, activities, agencies, and all other organizational entities that require access to DoD SAPs, pursuant to the terms and conditions of a memorandum of agreement, or other interagency agreement, established with the DoD.

3. <u>DEFINITIONS</u>. See Glossary.

4. <u>RESPONSIBILITIES</u>

    a. <u>Under Secretary of Defense for Intelligence (USD(I))</u>. The USD(I) shall function as the office of primary responsibility for the development and update of this Volume.

    b. <u>Heads of the DoD Components and OSD Principal Staff Assistants (PSAs)</u>. The Heads of the DoD Components and OSD PSAs with oversight or cognizant authority (CA) over SAPs shall develop and issue marking guidance for SAP material they create, receive, or secure as prescribed by this Volume.

5. <u>PROCEDURES</u>. Marking requirements and procedures for SAP information are detailed in Enclosures 2 through 6.

6. <u>RELEASABILITY</u>. ~~UNLIMITED. This Volume is approved for public release and is available on the Internet from the DoD Issuances Website at http://www.dtic.mil/whs/directives.~~ *Cleared for public release.* *This Volume is available on the Directives Division Website at http://www.esd.whs.mil/DD/.*

7. <u>EFFECTIVE DATE</u>. This Volume~~:~~ *is effective October 10, 2013.*

    ~~a. Is effective October 10, 2013.~~

    ~~b. Must be reissued, cancelled, or certified current within 5 years of its publication to be considered current in accordance with DoD Instruction 5025.01 (Reference (g)).~~

    ~~c. Will expire effective October 10, 2023 and be removed from the DoD Issuances Website if it hasn't been reissued or cancelled in accordance with Reference (g).~~

Michael G. Vickers
Under Secretary of Defense for
Intelligence

Enclosures
1. References
2. Basic Marking Guidance for DoD SAP Information
3. Applying the File Series Exemption (FSE) to SAP Documents
4. Marking Guidance for Disestablished SAPs
5. Marking Special Types of SAP Materials
6. Marking IS Storage Media Containing SAP Information
Glossary

TABLE OF CONTENTS

TABLE

FIGURES

20

ENCLOSURE 1

REFERENCES

(a) DoD Directive 5143.01, "Under Secretary of Defense for Intelligence (USD(I))," ~~November 23, 2005~~ *October 24, 2014, as amended*

(b) DoD Directive 5205.07, "Special Access Program (SAP) Policy," July 1, 2010

(c) Executive Order 13526, "Classified National Security Information," December 29, 2009

(d) Part 2001 subpart C of title 32, Code of Federal Regulations

(e) DoD Manual 5200.01, Volume 2, "Information Security Program: Marking of Classified Information," February 24, 2012, as amended

(f) Directive Type Memorandum 07-021, "Declassification Marking Guidance for DoD Special Access Program (SAP) Classified Material," April 26, 2007 (hereby cancelled)

~~(g) DoD Instruction 5025.01, "DoD Directives Program," September 26, 2012 as amended~~

(~~h~~g) DoD Instruction 5205.11, "Management, Administration, and Oversight of DoD Special Access Programs (SAPs)," February 6, 2013

(~~i~~h) Assistant to the President for National Security Affairs Memorandum, "Exemption of File Series from Automatic Declassification," March 30, 2005[1]

(~~j~~i) DoD Manual 5200.01, Volume 1, "Information Security Program: Overview, Classification, and Declassification," February 24, 2012

(~~k~~j) Section 3303 of chapter 33 of title 44, United States Code

~~(l) DoD Directive 5015.2, "DoD Records Management Program," March 6, 2000~~

(k) *DoD Instruction 5015.02, "DoD Records Management Program," February 24, 2015, as amended*

---

[1]The DoD SAPCO maintains a copy of Reference (~~h~~g).

ENCLOSURE 2

BASIC MARKING GUIDANCE FOR DoD SAP INFORMATION

1. GENERAL

a. SAP information shall be marked in accordance with the guidance contained herein, and this guidance shall be reflected in the security classification guide (SCG) developed for each program. The marking instructions discussed in this Volume are not all-inclusive, but do reflect the marking requirements for DoD SAP information required by References (c), (d), and (e).

b. An immediate re-marking effort for existing SAP documents, media, hardware, and other program-generated material is not required. However, if SAP documents are to be transferred or transmitted outside of a SAP facility, the custodian must re-mark the document(s) per the guidance herein, prior to dispatch. Program SCGs shall be modified to integrate guidance in this Volume during the guide's next periodic review or revision.

c. SAP material must be marked as soon as it is produced to notify the holder and recipients of its safeguarding requirements. Markings shall be uniformly and conspicuously applied to leave no doubt about the classified status of the information and the SAP protection required.

d. Marking challenges pertaining to SAP material shall be forwarded through the program security officer (PSO) to the CA Special Access Program Central Office (SAPCO). The CA SAPCO will coordinate with the SAP Original Classification Authority (OCA) as needed. Consideration and decisions regarding the removal of information from SAP controls requires coordination and approval in accordance with Enclosure 3 of DoD Instruction 5205.11 (Reference (hg)).

e. Deviations from prescribed SAP markings will be forwarded through the PSO for approval by the CA SAPCO.

2. SAP CONTROL MARKINGS

a. SAP control markings denote classified information that requires enhanced protection in accordance with Reference (b), section 4.3 of Reference (c), and Reference (hg). SAP information will be properly marked to reflect this status to the holder and shall include:

(1) The date and office of origin.

(2) The overall classification.

(3) CLASSIFIED BY: The classification authority and reason for classification (if originally classified).

(4) CLASSIFIED BY: The source (if derived). A document derivatively classified based on source documents marked "Multiple Sources" the derivative classifier shall cite the source documents.

(5) The SAP nickname or code word.

(6) Other assigned program identifier(s) (PID(s)).

(7) The portions that contain SAP information, dissemination controls, document control data (if required), and declassification instructions.

b. The level of classification (e.g., TOP SECRET) spelled out, the caveat "SPECIAL ACCESS REQUIRED" or the acronym "SAR," the program nickname (e.g., TAXI GREY) or code word (e.g., DAGGER), and the dissemination control (if assigned) shall be annotated on the banner line at the head and foot of each document page or media containing SAP information. Assigned PIDs (e.g., TG; RZD) shall not be used in the banner line. A hyphen (-) without interjected spaces shall be used to separate "SAR" and the program's nickname or code word. The banner line must be conspicuous enough to alert anyone handling the document that it contains SAP material (e.g., the font is larger or different than the font in normal text; or a contrasting color). The banner line must be constructed per the sequence or hierarchy reflected in the notes of the Table in this enclosure and Reference (e).

c. When information from three or more SAPs is included in a single document, indicate "MULTIPLE PROGRAMS" after SAR in the banner line (e.g. SECRET//SAR-MULTIPLE PROGRAMS) (see the Table). The term "Multiple Sources" is placed as the derivative classification instruction on the first page and these multiple sources are listed at the end of the document.

d. SAPs specifically exempted from normal congressional reporting requirements by the Secretary of Defense shall also be marked "WAIVED" in the banner line, at applicable portions, and prominently on media (e.g., TOP SECRET//SAR-DIGITAL AXIS//WAIVED). In such cases, "WAIVED" shall be placed last in the sequence and serves as a dissemination control marking.

e. Each paragraph shall be portion marked with the level of classification, "SAR", and the assigned PID (e.g., TS//SAR-TG). Use a hyphen without interjected spaces to separate the "SAR" caveat and the PID. The PID for each SAP mentioned must be cited in the portion marking, regardless of the total number of PIDs. Multiple PIDs must be listed in alphabetical order, separated from one another by a single forward slash (/), the "SAR" caveat and PID. If a dissemination control applies, such as waived (WAIVED), it will also be reflected at applicable portions or paragraphs (see the Table).

f. Document cover sheets shall not be annotated with classified code words.

g. Formal accountability measures described in Volume 1 of this Manual will be used to control the production and distribution of Top Secret SAP material. Hard copy documents containing Top Secret SAP information shall include in the lower right corner of each accountable page, the following: the assigned document control number (DCN), page number and total page count (page 1 of 8; page 2 of 8; etc.), and the copy number and total copies made (copy 2 of 4). When a controlled document (e.g., the original Copy 2) is reproduced, the new product may be marked "Copy 2A," indicating that Copy 2 has been copied one time, or it may be given a separate accountability number. Hardware and media shall be marked with the DCN and the copy number, if applicable.

Table. Examples of SAP Banner Line, Portion, and Dissemination Control Markings

Banner Line	Portion Markings
SECRET//SPECIAL ACCESS REQUIRED-TAXI GREY	(TS//SAR-TG)
SECRET//SAR-RAZOR DUST	(S//SAR-RZD)
SECRET//SAR-SWAGGER	(S//SAR-SGR)
SECRET//SAR-BLUE FOG/SAR-MUDDY PATH	(S//SAR-BFG/SAR-MDP)
TOP SECRET//SAR-MULTIPLE PROGRAMS*	(TS//SAR-TG/SAR-STK/SAR-BP)
TOP SECRET//SI-GAMMA//SAR-PRIOR TALLY	(TS//SI-G//SAR-PRT)
SECRET//SAR-FULL TILT	(S//SAR-FT)
TOP SECRET//SAR-DIGITAL AXIS//WAIVED	(TS//SAR-DGA//WAIVED)
TOP SECRET//SAR-ORION//WAIVED	(TS//SAR-ORN//WAIVED)
TOP SECRET//HCS//SAR-ZAPPER	(TS//HCS//SAR-ZPR)
TOP SECRET//TALENT KEYHOLE//SAR-STAGGER	(TS//TK//SAR-SGR)
TOP SECRET//SAR-TIN BAKER//WAIVED	(TS//SAR-TB//WAIVED)

Notes:
* Use "MULTIPLE PROGRAMS" in the banner line when 3 or more SAPs are referenced in the document. Use "MULTIPLE SOURCES" in the classification instructions on the first page of the document and include a list of these sources on the last page of the document.

Data hierarchy (left to right sequence) is: U.S. classification//Sensitive Compartmented Information (SCI) system(s)//SAP//Atomic Energy Act//Foreign Government Information// Dissemination Controls//Other Dissemination Controls.

The illustrative examples reflected in this table are UNCLASSIFIED.

   h. SAP information in digital format shall be subject to all requirements of Reference (e) and marked with proper classification markings to the extent that such marking is practical; including portion marking, overall classification, "classified by," "derived from" or "reason for classification," and "declassify on" (see Figure 1).

   i. Working papers containing SAP information shall be dated when created, marked, controlled, and safeguarded with the highest classification of any information contained therein. In accordance with Enclosure 3 of Reference (e), if these items are released by the originator outside the originating activity, retained more than 30 days from the date of origin, or filed permanently then they must be marked in the same manner prescribed for a finished document at the same classification level.

Figure 1. Marking Sample (Memorandum)

This Sample is UNCLASSIFIED – Markings are for Training Purposes ONLY

TOP SECRET//SAR-RED CAR/SAR-TIN BAKER//WAIVED

[Date of origin]

MEMORANDUM FOR SAP DOCUMENT PREPARERS

From: Director of SAPCO, MDA

SUBJECT: (U) Markings for a SAP Document

 (U//FOUO) This sample memorandum highlights markings for classified documents containing SAP information.

 (S//SAR-RC) This section demonstrates how to mark a paragraph that contains SAP information from one Secret program. The portion marking reflects the highest classification level in the portion or paragraph.

 (TS//SAR-RC/SAR-TBK//WAIVED) This section demonstrates how to mark a paragraph that contains SAP information from two programs. The portion marking reflects the highest classification level in the portion or paragraph. Additionally, since TBK is a Waived SAP, the dissemination control is also reflected in the portion marking.

 (U//FOUO) Portion markings for the Subject and Attachments indicate the classification of the subject or attachment title; not the classification of the document. Also note that Document Control information is reflected in the lower right corner for SAP documents requiring formal accountability.

Signature Block

Attachment:
Tab A: (U) Quad Chart

Classified by: David L. Smith, PSO
Derived from: RC SCG dated 20081128; TBK SCG dated 20090415
Declassify on: 20511231 (per FSE dated 20050330)

Upon Removal of Attachment(s), this Document is [Classification Level]

MDA SAPCO/0012-10
Page 1 of 2
Copy 1 of 4

TOP SECRET//SAR-RED CAR/SAR-TIN BAKER//WAIVED

ENCLOSURE 3

APPLYING THE FILE SERIES EXEMPTION (FSE) TO SAP DOCUMENTS

1. <u>GENERAL</u>. The marking guidance reflected in this enclosure applies to all documents containing DoD SAP information. As these documents are used (e.g., as a source of extracted SAP information, transmitted or moved from one location to another, re-introduced into the working environment from retired status, or modified from their existing state), they must be marked in accordance with the guidance in Figures 2 or 3 of this enclosure. All newly generated SAP documents will reflect markings that conform to this guidance.

2. <u>FSE</u>. SAPs established pursuant to Reference (b) have been granted an FSE in accordance with the Assistant to the President for National Security Affairs Memorandum (Reference (ih)). Reference (ih) exempts the file series of records related to DoD SAPs from automatic declassification at 25 years. SAP documents, dated prior to January 1, 1982, shall be declassified on December 31, 2021. SAP documents dated after January 1, 1982, shall be declassified on December 31 of the 40th year after the date of the document, unless it is reviewed and submitted for another extension. Requests for extensions will be submitted by the CA SAPCO to the DoD SAPCO, which, in accordance with Volume 1 of DoD Manual 5200.01 (Reference (ji)), must submit the request to the Information Security Oversight Office, National Archives and Records Administration, no less than 6 months before the declassification date.

Figure 2. <u>Markings for SAP Information Classified by an OCA</u>

FOR MATERIAL DATED PRIOR TO JANUARY 1, 1982
Classified by: Name and position; include agency if not apparent
Reason: 1.4 [list appropriate subparagraph(s): a-h]
Declassify on: 20211231 (per FSE dated 20050330)

FOR MATERIAL DATED ON OR AFTER JANUARY 1, 1982
Classified by: Name and position; include agency if not apparent
Reason: 1.4 [list appropriate subparagraph(s): a-h]
Declassify on: [insert December 31 of the year the document is 40 years old unless it is reviewed and submitted for another extension] (per FSE dated 20050330)

Figure 3. Markings for SAP Information That Is Derivatively Classified

---

FOR MATERIAL DATED PRIOR TO JANUARY 1, 1982

Classified by: Name and position; include agency if not apparent

Derived from: SCG, [date]; the source document subject, author and date; or Multiple Sources

Declassify on: 20211231 (per FSE dated 20050330)

FOR MATERIAL DATED ON OR AFTER JANUARY 1, 1982

Classified by: Name and position; include agency if not apparent

Derived from: SCG, [date]; the source document subject, author and date; or Multiple Sources

Declassify on: [insert December 31 of the year the document is 40 years old unless it is reviewed and submitted for another extension] (per FSE dated 20050330)

In accordance with Reference (e), if the classified information is derived from multiple sources, the classifier shall include a list of the source materials in, or attached to, each derivatively classified document.

ENCLOSURE 4

MARKING GUIDANCE FOR DISESTABLISHED SAPS

1. GENERAL. A disestablished SAP is one that is terminated as a SAP by the Secretary or Deputy Secretary of Defense.

2. MANDATORY MARKING ACTIONS. Personnel granted access to SAP material shall implement all mandatory marking actions prescribed in the program termination plan.

3. ADDITIONAL REQUIREMENTS. Marking requirements, beyond those cited in the termination plan, apply when:

a. A SAP has been terminated, but still requires SAP protections. For this condition:

(1) SAP markings shall not be altered and the document shall retain SAP protection requirements.

(2) When documents have been sealed in boxes or containers, or individual marking is otherwise costly and time consuming, a letter shall be affixed to the box or container that contains the correct marking instructions and declassification instructions. If affixing a letter to the box or container is inappropriate, then the letter will be retained by the responsible security officer, and the custodian will place a copy of the marking instructions in the first file inside the box when feasible.

b. SAP information completely transitions to non-SAP classified information. For this condition:

(1) Stripping a document of SAP protection or status may not change the document's classification level (Top Secret, Secret, Confidential) and protection measures required by Reference (e). When taking this action, the OCA must include these markings on the information: the level of classification, identification of the OCA, declassification instructions, a concise reason for continuing classification, and the date of the SAP termination action.

(2) SAP markings on the document (in the banner line and portion markings) shall be redacted or completely marked through and blacked out to reflect the loss of SAP status.

(3) Documents will be reviewed for declassification by the later standard of: December 31 of the fifth year following the removal of SAP protections; or December 31 of the year in which the records are 25 years old. If this declassification review is not performed, then the pertinent records shall be declassified automatically.

(4) Markings on data residing on electronic media shall be redacted or completely marked through and blacked out to reflect the loss of SAP status.

   c. DoD information from a disestablished DoD SAP that is shared with or transferred to non-DoD entities (e.g., Department of Homeland Security, or Director of National Intelligence) retains all other applicable markings for special handling. For this condition:

     (1) DoD SAP markings must be redacted to reflect the loss of DoD SAP status.

     (2) The material shall be protected and marked per the SCGs or jointly approved transition plan.

   d. When DoD SAP information is declassified, the overall classification markings that appear on all pages shall be redacted or completely marked through and blacked out and replaced with these markings: the word "Declassified," the identity (name and position) of the declassification authority, or the title and date of the declassification guide.

4. <u>RETENTION REVIEW</u>. Documents containing information from a disestablished DoD SAP shall be maintained in accordance with the applicable DoD Component's Records Management Manuals, as required by section 3303 of chapter 33 of title 44, United States Code (Reference (~~k~~*j*)) and ~~DoDD 5015.2~~ *DoDI 5015.02* (Reference (~~l~~*k*)).

ENCLOSURE 5

MARKING SPECIAL TYPES OF SAP MATERIALS

1. <u>GENERAL</u>. For general guidance regarding the marking of special type of materials, see Enclosure 3 of Reference (e). These procedures only address certain aspects that are unique to SAP materials.

2. <u>FILES, FOLDERS, OR GROUPS OF DOCUMENTS</u>. To prevent mishandling, these SAP materials shall be conspicuously marked with the highest classification and the PID of each SAP material contained therein.

3. <u>INFORMATION IN DIGITAL FORMAT</u>. See Enclosure 3 of Reference (e), "Marking in the Electronic Environment." Accountability controls for Top Secret SAP material are not required until the item is printed.

4. <u>FILM AND VIDEO</u>. These materials will have a lead-in header and run-out trailer of at least five seconds projecting the highest DoD classification, nickname(s) or code word(s) and handling caveats of SAP information contained therein. Additionally, the film canister or videocassette will be marked with the highest DoD classification, nickname(s) or PIDs, and handling caveats.

6. <u>OTHER ITEMS</u>. All other items containing SAP information shall be marked clearly with the applicable SAP control markings. These control markings shall be prominent and placed within or contiguous to the portion. Such markings shall be based on portion content alone with the classification symbol placed before the caption.

7. <u>INFORMATION SYSTEM (IS) HARDWARE</u>. Except as otherwise specified in this Volume, IS equipment that processes, conveys, or stores SAP information shall conspicuously bear a SAP control label (see Enclosure 6 of this Volume) or be permanently marked per the program SCG.

8. <u>SYSTEMS, SUB-SYSTEMS, AND PARTS</u>. Material that includes SAP systems, sub-systems, and parts shall be marked in a manner that will identify the classification and caveat for the item. If marking of the item is impractical, then a tag or other form of identification shall be attached. Consult the PSO when unusual situations arise regarding this type of marking.

ENCLOSURE 6

MARKING IS STORAGE MEDIA
CONTAINING SAP INFORMATION

1. <u>SOFTWARE-GENERATED MARKINGS</u>. Where practical, data owners will program the software of classified IS storing SAP information to mark each classified file stored in the system with the highest overall DoD classification level and all applicable control markings (i.e., in the same manner as other SAP items).

2. <u>REMOVABLE IS MEDIA</u>

    a. <u>General</u>. Removable IS storage media includes any device to which data may be written or upon which data may be stored that can be physically removed from a system by the user or operator. Removable IS storage media shall be marked with a SAP control marking if the media has ever been used on a IS system that processes SAP information, and the media was in a "writable" "vice read only" condition.

    b. <u>External Markings</u>. In addition to proper classification markings in accordance with Reference (e), the media shall be marked with the nickname(s) or assigned PIDs, and SAR handling caveats as appropriate. Ensure that the markings are affixed to the media, not an interchangeable carrier (e.g., physically label the compact disc (CD) or hard disk).

        (1) The SF 712 label is required for all media containing SCI. If SCI and SAP information reside on the same disk or removable drive, it is permissible to cut one label (e.g., SECRET or TOP SECRET), add SAR-PID, and place it on the SCI label to show that the media contains both SCI and SAP.

        (2) The purple classified media label (SF 709) is NOT authorized for use with DoD SAP media.

        (3) The "Data Descriptor" media label (SF 711) or a locally produced label must be used in addition to other labels to show the DCN, copy number, page number, handling restrictions, media contents, and office identifier. There are blocks on the SF 711 for classification, PIDs, and code words.

3. <u>NON-REMOVABLE IS MEDIA</u>

    a. Non-removable IS storage media includes any device processing or storing SAP data that is accessible only via the removal of computer panels or the application of hand tools. Examples include hard drives internal to a central processing unit.

b. All IS hardware containing non-removable computer media shall bear external labels indicating the applicable SAP control markings, including handling caveats and dissemination controls. If the media is removed for maintenance or disposal, appropriate SAP controls shall be applied.

GLOSSARY

PART I. ABBREVIATIONS AND ACRONYMS

CA	cognizant authority
CD	compact disc
DCN	document control number
DoDD	DoD Directive
FSE	file series exemption
IS	information system
OCA	original classification authority
PID	program identifier
PSA	principal staff assistant
PSO	program security officer
SAP	Special Access Program
SAPCO	Special Access Program Central Office
SAR	special access required
SCG	security classification guide
SCI	Sensitive Compartmented Information
SF	standard form
USD(I)	Under Secretary of Defense for Intelligence

PART II. DEFINITIONS

Unless otherwise noted, these terms and their definitions are for the purposes of this Volume.

banner line. A display or listing at the top and bottom of a document page that conveys the highest classification level of information contained in the document and the most restrictive control markings applicable to the overall document.

code word. A single word assigned to a SAP with a classified meaning (Confidential or higher), once activated by appropriate authority, to emphasize the required degree of security and to safeguard information pertaining to SAPs.

derivative classification. Defined in Reference (e).

dissemination control markings. Defined in Reference (e).

<u>FSE</u>. An exception to the 25-year automatic declassification provisions of Reference (c). It applies to entire blocks of records replete with exemptible information, e.g., a "file series" of agency records bearing a similar subject or category association.

<u>IS</u>. Any telecommunications, or computer-related equipment, interconnected system or subsystems of equipment that is used in the acquisition, storage, manipulation, management, movement, control, display, switching, interchange, transmission, or reception of voice or data (digital or analog); includes software, firmware, and hardware.

<u>nickname</u>. Two separate unclassified words that are used in combination to represent a specific SAP or portion thereof.

<u>original classification.</u> Defined in Reference (e).

<u>PID</u>. Defined in Reference (hg).

<u>portion marking</u>. Using classification identifiers to independently mark sections, parts, or paragraphs as classified material. The classification of each portion depends solely upon the content of that portion. Portion markings shall be placed immediately preceding the material or data to remove any doubt as to the classification of a particular portion.

<u>PSA</u>. The Under Secretaries of Defense for Acquisition, Technology and Logistics, Policy, and Intelligence are examples of designated PSAs in support of the Secretary of Defense.

<u>SAP</u>. Defined in Reference (e).

<u>SAP facility</u>. A specific physical space that has been formally accredited in writing by the cognizant PSO that satisfies the criteria for generating, safeguarding, handling, discussing, and storing classified or unclassified program information, hardware, and materials.

<u>SCI</u>. Defined in Reference (e).

Made in the USA
Middletown, DE
05 July 2020